The Outdoor Lighting Pattern Book

Russell P. Leslie

Paula A. Rodgers

LIGHTING RESEARCH CENTER
Rensselaer Polytechnic Institute

Editing by Kevin Heslin

McGraw-Hill

New York • San Francisco • Washington, D.C • Auckland • Bogotá
Caracas • Lisbon • London • Madrid • Mexico City • Milan
Montreal • New Delhi • San Juan • Singapore
Sydney • Tokyo • Toronto

Rensselaer Polytechnic Institute, Troy, NY

Library of Congress Cataloging-in Publication Data

Leslie, Russell P.
    The outdoor lighting pattern book/Russell P. Leslie, Paula A.
Rodgers; the Lighting Research Center; editing by Kevin Heslin.
        p. cm.
    Includes index.
    ISBN 0–07–037188–1
    1. Exterior lighting. 2. Electric lighting. I. Rodgers, Paula
A. II. Heslin, Kevin. III. Rensselaer Polytechnic Institute.
Lighting Research Center. IV. Title.
TK4188.L45 1996   96–41377
621.32'29—DC20   CIP

McGraw·Hill
A Division of The McGraw·Hill Companies   **Rensselaer**   **LRC**
                                                                        Lighting Research Center

01 00 99 98 97 96   3 2 1

ISBN 0 07 037188-1

Library of Congress Card Catalog Number 96-41377

McGraw-Hill books are available at special quantity discounts to use as premiums and sales
promotions, or for use in corporate training programs. For more information, please write to the
Director of Special Sales, McGraw-Hill, 11 West 19th Street, New York, NY 10011 or contact
your local bookstore.

No lighting plan has the power to prevent a criminal act. Opinions represented in this
publication are based on the assumption that increased lighting may provide more security
in some areas than would otherwise occur.

Contents

Sponsors

Consolidated Edison Company of New York, Inc.

Empire State Electric Energy Research Corporation

New York State Energy Research and Development Authority

Niagara Mohawk Power Corporation

Northeast Utilities

Northern States Power Company

Lighting Equipment Manufacturers Who Supported The Outdoor Lighting Pattern Book *Through Lighting Research Center Partnership*

Eagle Electric Manufacturing Co., Inc.

GE Lighting

The Genlyte Group
  Hadco • Stonco • Wide-Lite

MagneTek

OSRAM SYLVANIA INC.

Philips Lighting

Other Lighting Research Center Partners

Bonneville Power Administration

NUTEK

U.S. Environmental Protection Agency

Acknowledgments

We are particularly indebted to the following sponsors of *The Outdoor Lighting Pattern Book* and their representatives: Consolidated Edison Company of New York (Janet Crawford; Peter J. Jacobson; Arthur Kressner; Frank X. Lutz, P.E.; Michael A. Maher; and Peter Shulhof), Empire State Electric Energy Research Corporation (Eileen McCaffrey, Eric Neumann, Frank E. Porretto, and Edward A. Torrero), New York State Energy Research and Development Authority (Marsha L. Walton), Niagara Mohawk Power Corporation, Northeast Utilities (Paul Kuehn, Peter Morante, Sharon Flannery), Northern States Power Company (Ron Hammer), and Rensselaer's Lighting Research Center (Mark S. Rea).

These sponsors, Con Edison in particular, helped us initiate *The Outdoor Lighting Pattern Book* and contributed ideas towards its development. We also acknowledge the many other representatives of the sponsors who helped in countless ways, big and small.

We also thank Peter Boyce, Barbara J. Hamilton, Kevin Heslin, Maarten Mulder, and Pamela Horner, who with the authors formed the project team and expert panel. In addition, Boyce patiently guided our development and application of lighting evaluation criteria. Mulder ran endless AGI lighting simulations, and when not otherwise occupied, organized and updated spreadsheets containing all the pertinent research and economic data developed in this project. Horner contributed invaluable field experience in the development and evaluation of base cases and lighting designs and knowledge about the equipment used in each. She also developed the glossary and conducted the roundtables organized to critique the book at each stage. Naomi Miller reviewed every preliminary design, threw out many, and taught us a lot.

Neil H. Eklund worked on the field studies and data analysis. Other LRC contributors and reviewers were Judith Block, Howard Brandston, Lisa Bruno, Joseph Ceterski, Kathryn M. Conway, Robert Davis, Amy L. Fowler, Erika Gillmeister, James J. Gross, Claudia Hunter, Yunfen Ji, Catherine Luo, Dorene Maniccia, Karen Pero, Carrie Saalfield, and Jason Teague.

Outside reviewers whose comments and suggestions strengthened the book include Bill Blitzer and Rod Stummer from the Genlyte Group, Glen Krueger, Rick Leeds, and the dozens of architects, engineers, facility managers, community leaders, and utility representatives who attended roundtables or spent a cold winter's night evaluating sites in New York City. Particularly hardy and helpful in this regard were Con Edison's Energy Services staff and Certified Contractors.

We gratefully acknowledge HMC Group Ltd.'s design and production efforts, Mark Patrizio's skillfully and carefully drawn site illustrations and Kaiser Illustration's line drawings of lamps, luminaires, and controls. We also thank Nager Reynolds for their contributions to the cover design. The formidable task of indexing *The Outdoor Lighting Pattren Book* was undertaken ably by Robert Richardson.

Foreword

It is hard to imagine an architectural space today that would not have some lighting as part of its design. However, the driving forces behind these designs have changed dramatically in the last quarter century. In the 1970s the American people first became aware that the supply of nonrenewable energy resources was dwindling. Consumers and producers examined the energy efficiency of every product and every manufacturing process, in the process developing new and revised methods of reducing energy consumption.

The lighting industry participated fully by developing new energy-efficient light sources and helping to write new practice guidelines and standards that called for better and more effective use of light. State and local officials often incorporated these developments in building and energy codes that limited the use of electricity for lighting. Today, the lighting industry continues to develop ever more energy-efficient products and practices.

In the 1990s, Americans have focused on different problems: crime and the economy. In recent elections, politicians across the country have vied to take the toughest stance on crime to capitalize on the public's fear of crime. Many of them also have played to the public's well-founded economic insecurity.

The solutions to these problems will not all be well publicized or dramatic. Ordinary people from every walk of life, business and neighborhood leaders, have begun to seek solutions on their own. The important and underutilized qualities of lighting make it a major part of efforts to fight crime and boost economies. Lighting can make places feel welcoming, comfortable, and safe to visit. Lighting can call attention to shop windows and merchandise. Lighting can increase sales and productivity. The ability to see well adds the dimension of security to night experiences. Lighting is a good investment: the cost to design and install lighting is low compared to other construction costs.

The Outdoor Lighting Pattern Book is a tool to help realize the greatest benefit from an investment in lighting. It is the second publication of this type from the Lighting Research Center at Rensselaer Polytechnic Institute in Troy, NY. The first, *The Lighting Pattern Book for Homes*, helped people so much that the Lighting Research Center and the book's sponsors decided that a similar publication on outdoor lighting was at once required. *The Outdoor Lighting Pattern Book* is a tool to assist nonprofessionals achieve good lighting solutions.

The lighting patterns illustrated within this book provide quality, energy-efficient lighting solutions for areas ranging in size and variety from neighborhood streets to residential buildings to commercial districts to public places. Readers who are interested can also find a description of the principles of good lighting practice and how to predict the economic benefit of their investment. The book is an excellent guide that will lend direction and instruction to improve the aesthetic appearance of projects that it sheds light on.

The Outdoor Lighting Pattern Book can be used as a way to improve the appearance of outdoor areas, increase the security of a site, and boost pedestrian use of retail areas and parks and so increase the value of property. I am proud to have been a small part of the creation of *The Outdoor Lighting Pattern Book*, and I encourage all to put it to work.

Howard Brandston, FIES, FIALD, FCIBSE

Preface

For years I struggled to make it easier for all of us to enjoy the benefits that come with good lighting. I've thought about how lighting experts can best provide accurate and understandable information to people and companies that light acres and acres of our environment. Ideally, each installation would receive the careful consideration of a professional lighting designer. But at most installations, people with little or no formal lighting training design and specify the lighting system.

I've been exploring lighting patterns as a way to help these people specify lighting systems in an environmentally responsible way that meets their design criteria for comfort, appearance, and cost. These lighting patterns can serve as templates for lighting specifiers. I believe that specifiers will be prepared to make better lighting decisions if they have easy-to-use patterns and pertinent information to help them achieve their lighting objectives.

In 1993, the Lighting Research Center published *The Lighting Pattern Book for Homes*, which I wrote with Kathryn M. Conway to bring patterns to those who select lighting for homes. Since then, the LRC has been approached by leading electric utilities and government groups asking for patterns for other applications. We planned *The Outdoor Lighting Pattern Book* to meet these requests.

I believe we should celebrate the potential of outdoor lighting: nothing shapes our nighttime visual experience as powerfully as lighting. The time is right for each of us to examine our use of lighting. Modern lighting hardware lights more effectively than older equipment and uses energy more efficiently. Communities are increasingly using lighting to create stronger identities or to discourage crime. Retailers hope to increase sales using lighting. In addition, some electric utilities offer outdoor lighting programs to assist their customers. But we know that the indiscriminate or inappropriate use of lighting incurs environmental penalties such as increased emissions from power plants, light trespass, and light pollution.

I wanted to be certain that these outdoor lighting patterns considered the relevant perspectives: aesthetics, technology, human factors, energy, vision, economics, installation, and maintenance. Paula Rodgers, an experienced outdoor lighting designer, brought her expertise to our multi-disciplinary project team. The project team struggled, debated, laughed, struggled some more, and finally agreed on methods to rate lighting designs for appearance, security, and economics. These methods were not arbitrary. They were based on extensive research reviews and new laboratory and field studies that we conducted.

These outdoor lighting patterns survived our evaluation sessions, external reviews, and critiques from the intended audience: electricians, utility representatives, community groups, facility managers, architects, and engineers. After each review we improved the patterns. They are now a good starting point for design planning. We hope these patterns will facilitate your contribution to environmentally responsible, quality outdoor lighting.

Russell P. Leslie, AIA, IES

To me, the purpose of lighting patterns and the essence of *The Outdoor Lighting Pattern Book* can be summarized in the adage a picture is worth a thousand words. Most people have trouble visualizing an outdoor lighting scene, especially when they are equipped only with photocopies of luminaire catalog sheets and a site plan that uses little dots to represent luminaires. As a consultant and lighting designer, I found it hard to convey lighting concepts to clients without perspectives and site plans that I shaded to show the distribution of light. This practical experience explains my enthusiasm for *The Outdoor Lighting Pattern Book:* how wonderful to have so many illustrations of outdoor lighting and to show clients sites like their very own, complete with light levels and cost information, plus ratings of how it looks and whether people would likely feel safe there. Such a resource would have helped me a lot.

I think of *The Outdoor Lighting Pattern Book* as two tools in one. For those who have little or no experience in outdoor lighting, the book is a place to start looking for outdoor lighting concepts, an idea book. For those who need to convey lighting concepts to a client, the book is a ready set of illustrations that depict outdoor lighting concepts and principles. *The Outdoor Lighting Pattern Book* is a powerful and convenient way to communicate the possibilities of outdoor lighting.

Paula A. Rodgers, IES

The Outdoor Lighting Pattern Book

PRINCIPLES

The *Outdoor Lighting Pattern Book* addresses many of the challenges inherent in designing lighting for outdoor areas. The designs in the book have been developed to be consistent with the principles of lighting and vision, each of which has a terminology, or jargon, of its own. A novice to lighting can follow the logic of the designs, but a better understanding of the principles and the glossary (p.199) can be useful when adapting the designs to real situations.

Designers and specifiers who create successful lighting designs clearly identify objectives and understand how to use light to meet these objectives. Most outdoor lighting designs are meant to

- enhance the safety of people and the security of property,

- establish and maintain suitable aesthetics, and

- deliver a lighting installation within appropriate budgets for equipment, installation, operation, and maintenance.

Not all these objectives are equally important in every application: they may even conflict in some. For example, in a secured storage area that is not used after dark, appearance may be a very low priority. Furthermore, methods of minimizing costs may conflict with the objective of protecting people or property. Even minimizing equipment costs may conflict with achieving low operating costs. The designer starts the design process by identifying and prioritizing objectives.

Illuminance (measured in footcandles or lux) is the characteristic of light most important to lighting specifiers. Unless glare interferes, people always see better with more light; they can respond faster and have better acuity and color vision.

People do not see illuminance; rather, they see light after it meets a surface and reflects off it. The light reflected from a surface is called luminance. A white concrete parking lot will reflect more light than will a black asphalt lot with the same lighting installation and have a higher luminance. Therefore people will see better in the concrete parking lot than in the asphalt parking lot.

Outdoor installations where the average illuminance is more than ten times the minimum illuminance can be problematic. Poor luminaire placement and objects can combine to cause shadows or relative bright areas so that illuminance is not uniform. Non-uniform illuminance can impair people's ability to see clearly at a distance, limiting their time to respond to activity around them. Non-uniform lighting can also introduce confusing or false information. For example, shadows may be interpreted as edges.

Contrast, which is the relative luminance of an object against its immediate background, is also important to lighting specifiers. Designers can select materials to enhance or minimize luminance contrast. For example, a white concrete curb against a black asphalt pavement provides a higher luminance contrast than it would against a concrete pavement. Paint can also increase luminance contrast. For example, the edge of a loading bay can be given a greater contrast by painting a white line along it.

Other factors also influence vision, many of which are difficult to predict during design. For example, the size of an object affects its visibility; smaller objects are harder to see. Readaptation affects visibility; if a person leaves a brightly lit interior space, he or she will require a few moments to be able to see well in the darker outdoors.

Keeping People Safe and Property Secure

Security lighting must enable people to take action at a distance. People must see what is happening around them in time to respond. When people can see far ahead and into any potential hiding places as well as identify escape paths if necessary, they may feel more secure and become more likely to enter an area and remain awhile. Their presence can encourage others to do the same. The visibility provided by lighting not only encourages use of an area, which can prevent some crimes, it acts as a deterrent to would-be criminals who wish to go unseen. After a crime, good lighting helps witnesses to describe and identify criminals.

Security lighting should also protect property. Lighting can enhance the security of property in three different ways. The most common security lighting approach uses a lot of light to try to illuminate the whole area to be secured. This approach reduces shadows and dark areas, making people inside the area visible to observers outside and within the area. A parking lot lighted uniformly brighter than adjoining properties uses this strategy; people can easily be seen approaching any car. Besides better visibility, a lot of light can be a deterrent by making the statement that a site is protected. To make an effective statement, the lighting must appear brighter than the surrounding area: a rule of thumb is that the average illuminance in the enclosed area should be at least twice that in surrounding areas. Criminals avoid the parking lot knowing that they can be easily seen.

Glare reduces visibility. For example, people have trouble seeing the roadway when looking into oncoming headlights. Low-mounted luminaires aimed out of a guarded storage area or similar facility will create glare that can blind potential trespassers, making them uncertain about what is in the area and how well it is guarded. Potential criminals may also recognize that they might be seen from inside by security cameras or guards. To make the glare strategy effective, the secure area should be left dark and the low-mounted luminaires should floodlight all the approaches to the area.

In a no-light strategy, security can be enhanced because the area goes unnoticed; however, trespassers are equally hard to detect. Vandals may bypass an unlighted storage yard along a highway, but if they do notice it, the police will not see them at work. No-light strategies do nothing to increase a person's sense of security or ability to take action at a distance.

The effectiveness of a no-light strategy can be improved by using motion sensors. The area remains dark to avoid attention, but if someone does approach, the motion sensors switch the lights on, drawing immediate attention. The intruder gets a strong cue that the area is watched.

When implementing the most common of these security lighting strategies—a lot of light—the most frequently asked question is how much light is enough. The quick and simple answer: a guideline developed from research at the Lighting Research Center (LRC) is to provide around 3 footcandles of illuminance throughout the area with no point less than 0.3 footcandles.

The LRC tested the long-standing belief that people experience a greater sense of security as light increases. Dr. Peter Boyce took two groups of observers to 27 commercial and residential sites in Albany and New York City. At each site, the observers rated the securi-

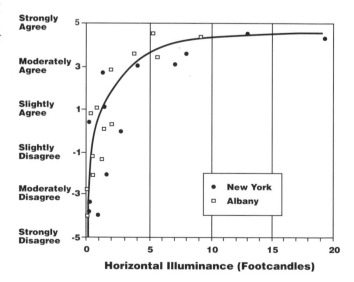

The relationship of horizontal illuminance to the average survey response of subjects for each outdoor site. Subjects assigned a score from –5 (strongly disagree) to +5 (strongly agree) to the statement: "This is a good example of security lighting."

ty provided by the lighting. The figure shows the relationship between the average horizontal illuminances at each site and the average ratings of the lighting. The ratings were higher for the sites with higher illuminance, but above about 3 footcandles, the improvement was slight. The relationship between horizontal illuminance and average ratings applied well to New York City and Albany despite the many differences between the two cities, implying that the guideline is applicable to many other locations.

Light source is another practical consideration. Metal halide and high pressure sodium are the two most common sources used for outdoor security lighting. Research by Dr. Mark Rea at the LRC shows that, at 3 footcandles or less, areas appear clearer and brighter when lighted with metal halide than when lighted with high pressure sodium, and color perception is better, too. However, high pressure sodium has longer life and undergoes less color shift than metal halide.

Dr. Rea's research has profound implications for the importance of lamp spectra in security applications. He has demonstrated that under illuminances less than 3 footcandles, which is typical of many outdoor applications, the eye's sensitivity shifts for off-axis tasks. Searching an area for a person in hiding, which is done with the periphery of the visual field, is one such task.

The sensitivity shift favors lamps that have more blue and green in their spectra. For example, a metal halide lamp may be 25-50 percent more effective than a high pressure sodium lamp for these tasks, but there would be no advantage for tasks such as reading a newspaper. Since many security-related visual tasks begin off-axis, security installations may be able to provide greater visibility under metal halide than under high pressure sodium lamps of the same wattage. Alternatively, equal visibility could be provided with lower-wattage metal halide lamps. These findings may prompt manufacturers to develop new light sources that take advantage of these findings.

The LRC also examined the effect of lamp spectra on the ability of witnesses to describe clothing, vehicles, or objects. Subjects in a test used color to describe a simulated crime scene. They tried to identify colors under different light sources at three different illuminances: 0.1, 1, and 10 footcandles.

The results show that people's ability to identify color suffers under light from low pressure sodium lamps at any illuminance and under light from high pressure sodium lamps at light levels below 1 footcandle. Above 10 footcandles, high pressure sodium is adequate for color discrimination by witnesses, but not as good as metal halide. Metal halide performs similarly to fluorescent and incandescent lamps even at illuminances as low as 0.1 footcandles. To the designer, this means that for witness identification, metal halide always has an advantage over high pressure sodium. The advantage increases as illuminance drops from 10 footcandles.

Improving Aesthetics

When designing an outdoor area to be an attractive place to be at night, the appearance of the people and features within it is particularly important. The lighting should support the design concept of the area, provide orientation, and be comfortable. Light should reveal the surroundings, but the designer should save the higher illuminances for highlighting paths, signs, building facades, foliage, and landscape features. The designer should also consider the color of the light source, glare, the appearance of luminaires, and the match of the luminaires to the site.

A lamp's ability to render color affects the appearance of people and objects, but choosing appropriate lamps depends on the reflective properties of the objects and how important it is for people to see skin tones that appear natural. No lamp is perfect for all situations. For example, high pressure sodium lamps reveal the color of red or yellow brick but mar the appearance of grass. Incandescent lamps flatter skin tones but are expensive to operate. Specifiers should try to select lamps with high color rendering indexes.

Direct glare is uncomfortable and distracting, and makes it difficult to see. When selecting a luminaire, the specifier should usually select a shielded luminaire and position it carefully. Shielded luminaires direct light downward. Luminaires that allow light to escape towards the sky contribute to light pollution and sky glow, which obscure the views of the sky at night. Some communities have enacted ordinances to limit light pollution and to restrict light trespass, which is light falling on adjoining properties. Unshielded luminaires are useful for lighting people's faces and other vertical surfaces such as building facades. Some designers use unshielded luminaires to attract attention to an area and let people know it is highly illuminated, but such approaches must be carefully balanced with glare considerations.

The luminaires are architectural elements, seen both day and night, so their appearance and style should support the design concept. Some applications may call for the designer to limit lighting to a few well-chosen areas. For example, the ball fields and lawns of a park may be dark, while the paths and foliage are lighted. The design will be more economical to install, operate, and maintain, although it will provide less security for the lawns. The design may also enhance the ambiance of the park by creating cozy, quiet areas.

A good match of the light to the site will define a circulation pattern, emphasize aesthetic features, and contribute to the attractiveness of the space. A poor match to the site will light inappropriate places such as an unsightly wall or a bedroom window and reduce the likelihood that a space will function as planned.

Minimizing costs

A lighting design that improves the safety, security, and appearance of an area may require much equipment and operate long hours. However, good lighting can produce benefits that outweigh the costs of a lighting installation.

The annual operating costs of the lighting installations in this book with the highest security ratings average $0.08 to $0.10 per square foot more than the installations with the poorest ratings, and the initial equipment costs are $0.50 to $1.00 more per square foot. Installation costs are roughly equal to the equipment costs, but whether these modest costs are worthwhile depends on which benefits are most desired.

Good security lighting may help reduce vandalism, improve the effectiveness of other measures, and help control liability and accident expenses. Well-designed lighting may bring other positive benefits such as increased sales and improved quality of life. Lighting designers can propose designs that include both cost and benefit information and help the client match the design solution to the design objectives.

First cost, annual maintenance cost, and annual energy costs should be considered in design proposals. First cost includes the cost of the lamps, luminaires, ballasts, controls, poles, wiring, and installation. First cost can sometimes be reduced by re-using existing poles and wiring. Annual maintenance costs are the annual labor and material costs of replacing lamps, ballasts, and controls. Long-life light sources, such as fluorescent, metal halide, and high pressure sodium lamps offer savings on lamp replacement costs, including labor.

Annual energy cost is the cost of the electricity used to operate the lighting systems. Energy savings can often be used to offset the first cost of energy-efficient lighting equipment. Energy savings result from choosing efficient lamps, using controls to turn off lamps when light is not needed, and selecting luminaires that direct light only where it is needed.

Failed or vandalized lamps and luminaires lower average illuminance and reduce the uniformity of light distribution and the extent of coverage. A maintenance program that includes scheduled replacement of lamps and cleaning of luminaires ensures that a successful lighting design will continue to meet its design objectives.

The designs and evaluations in *The Outdoor Lighting Pattern Book* consider the uses of the illustrated areas and offer ways to balance safety, security, appearance, and economy.

USING PATTERNS

The *Outdoor Lighting Pattern Book* has been developed to help bring purpose and design to everyday lighting plans. The model lighting plans, or patterns, modify familiar spaces and building types with lighting designs that have been evaluated using calculations, general principles, and expert opinions. These patterns provide objective design and application guidelines that differentiate alternative lighting schemes.

The patterns in *The Outdoor Lighting Pattern Book* are representations of places found in many towns and cities. Utility personnel, electrical contractors, neighborhood representatives, and even police officers critiqued preliminary sketches and photographs from the Lighting Research Center to ensure that the architecture, uses, and lighting of each pattern would be familiar to lighting specifiers from diverse communities. *The Outdoor Lighting Pattern Book* also includes fundamental information about lamps and luminaires.

A panel of lighting design, applications, and human factors experts evaluated each design and design alternatives prepared by qualified lighting design professionals for security, appearance, and annual operating costs. The panelists used their knowledge of design, equipment, and common practice to devise criteria for judging the appropriateness of each pattern as well as the suitability and the performance of the lighting. The panel supplemented its knowledge of outdoor lighting by conducting research into the relationship between lighting and the sense of security.

The expert panel also used a computer program, AGI (Advanced Graphical Interface) from Lighting Analysts, Inc., to simulate each lighting design. The program calculated values for horizontal illuminance, vertical illuminance, uniformity, and coverage that the panel used, along with color rendering index.

Guide to Patterns

Each pattern begins with a page that includes basic information about a site, summarizes the performance of each design, and includes a site plan that has been shaded to show the area included in cost and security evaluations. The next page shows how the space typically is lighted and includes information about the performance of the lighting system. The remaining pages reveal lighting upgrades and redesigns, prepared by a panel of lighting design, application, and human factors experts.

The **typical** designs represent lighting as it is found in many of our cities and towns. **Upgrades** are improved lighting designs that use the electrical boxes, poles, luminaires, and other lighting hardware found in the typical designs, where possible. Upgrades provide good advice for improving existing installations.

Outdoor lighting patterns provide basic site information on the first page. A shaded area on the site plan indicates the area of calculation for all costs, horizontal illuminance, and connected load.

Artist's Sketch

Site Plan

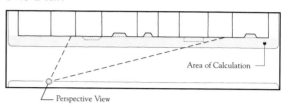

Easy-to-use tables summarize sense of security and appearance ratings, initial equipment costs, and annual costs for each typical, upgrade, and redesign.*

Summary Table

	Sense of Security	Appearance	Initial Equipment Cost	Annual Cost	
				Maintenance	Energy
Typical (p. 14)	★★	★	—	—	—
Upgrade (p. 15)	★★★★	★★★	$3000	$140	$660
Redesign 1 (p. 16)	★★★★	★★★	$5000	$67	$490
Redesign 2 (p. 16)	★★★★	★★★★	$5100	$130	$500

Key: ★ Poorest   ★★★★★ Best

* Existing street lights are excluded from all cost calculations.

Shaded sketches depict the effects of light and the positions of luminaires used in designs on the following pages. Icons and keys identify lamps and luminaires and provide cross references to chapters describing those technologies.

Artist's Shaded Sketch

Shaded Site Plan

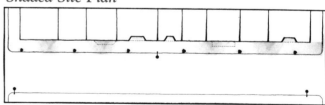

Icons and Keys

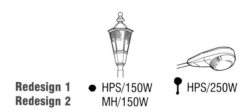

Redesign 1   ● HPS/150W   ♀ HPS/250W
Redesign 2   MH/150W

The expert panel evaluated each design on sense of security and appearance criteria. The project team estimated initial equipment costs, annual costs, average horizontal illuminances, and connected loads.* These designs are all within the power density allowance described in ASHRAE/IES 90.1-1989.

Security, Appearance, and Cost Evaluations

	Sense of Security	Appearance	Initial Equipment Cost	Annual Cost		Average Horizontal Illuminance	Connected Load
				Maintenance	Energy		
Redesign 1	★★★★	★★★	$5000	$67	$490	2.2 fc	1100 W
Redesign 2	★★★★	★★★★	$5100	$130	$500	2.0 fc	1100 W

Redesigns offer fresh lighting solutions not restricted by the locations of lighting hardware found in the typical design. Redesigns may be the best choice for renovations and new construction. Upgrades and redesigns show the effects of changing luminaires, lamps, and controls.

All the upgrades and redesigns use energy wisely and are within the power density allowances of ASHRAE/IES 90.1-1989, the industry standard published by the American Society of Heating, Refrigeration and Air-Conditioning Engineers and the Illuminating Engineering Society of North America (IESNA). The IESNA illuminance recommendations were considered, where applicable, in the upgrades and redesigns.

Shaded sketches provide an artist's interpretation of each area, how it has been lighted, and the appearance and positions of the luminaires. A site plan and icons detail the locations, types, and light distributions of the luminaires and lamps in each design. The site plans cannot be used to estimate illuminance but do indicate uniformity well.

The designs use generic versions of luminaires available from many manufacturers and distributors, and manufacturers make a wide variety of luminaires in each category. A lighting designer can help pick luminaires that complement an outdoor area and provide similar light distribution to that of the generic luminaires in the patterns.

A table at the bottom of each page provides the sense of security and appearance evaluations of the expert panel, and the initial equipment and annual operating costs for the design on that page.

Security and Appearance Ratings

The expert panel considered horizontal illuminance, vertical illuminance, uniformity, and coverage, along with color properties of the lamps, to rate the sense of security each design might generate. Five stars is the best rating, one star the poorest.

The expert panel also assigned a rating for the appearance of the lighting. Again the most-pleasing designs rate five stars. The panel considered the color properties of the lamps, the luminaires, the match to site, and glare.

A table summarizing each design lists the average horizontal illuminance for the area of calculation (the shaded area on the site plan). Horizontal illuminance is the amount of light (measured in footcandles) that falls on a horizontal plane or surface. The table also lists connected load in watts, the total power needed to operate all of the lighting in the design, except street lighting.

Costs

The Outdoor Lighting Pattern Book includes calculated initial equipment and annual operating costs for each design. The costs do not include existing street lights since they remain in all designs. Annual costs include maintenance and energy. For quick estimating installation costs are roughly equal to equipment costs. The Economics chapter includes equipment costs and the spreadsheet used in making cost calculations. A contractor can estimate the initial costs of the planned outdoor lighting systems.

Annual maintenance cost includes the prorated annual labor and material costs of replacing the lamps.

Energy cost is the product of the electric rate, the connected load, and the annual hours of operation. The annual energy cost to operate the lighting system is based on a rate of $0.10/kWh. A simple multiplier can adjust the energy costs if the local rate is higher or lower. All the lamps operate an average of 12 hours per day, unless noted in the description.

Consider these patterns as prototypes. Once you have identified the suitable pattern or patterns, engage a qualified lighting professional to adapt these patterns to your own projects. The relative importance you attach to security, appearance, and costs can help match your design objectives to your design solutions.

PATTERNS

The following 31 scenes resemble sites found in many of our cities, towns, and neighborhoods. Each scene shows the way these sites are typically lighted along with several improved designs developed by a team of lighting experts. The 31 scenes and the upgrades and redesigns, 82 in all, have been evaluated for security, appearance, and cost. To start planning a design, find the scenes that most resemble the areas to be lighted. This chapter then can help you quickly identify some appropriate lighting designs. The relative benefits of each approach should guide design decisions. In each of the lighting designs, the lamps, luminaires, controls, mounting equipment, and their locations have been identified to guide the adaptation of these designs to specific sites and objectives. These designs make use of generic products, so when adapting the designs, the designer must be sure to select products that perform similarly by using the Lamps, Luminaires, and Controls chapters.

Table of Contents

NEIGHBORHOOD SHOPPING

R etail shops line the blocks of many urban neighborhoods. The storefronts often have awnings, recessed entries, or overhangs, giving each shop its own appearance. Other businesses and residences occupy the upper floors.

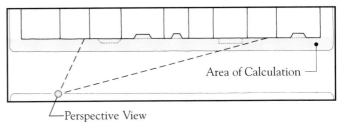

Area of Calculation

Perspective View

	Sense of Security	Appearance	Initial Equipment Cost	Annual Cost	
				Maintenance	Energy
Typical (p. 14)	★★	★	—	—	—
Upgrade (p. 15)	★★★★	★★★	$3000	$140	$660
Redesign 1 (p. 16)	★★★★	★★★	$5000	$67	$490
Redesign 2 (p. 16)	★★★★	★★★★	$5100	$130	$500

Key: ★ Poorest ★★★★★ Best

Typical

Three cobraheads, each mounted on a 35-ft pole, provide street lighting using one 250-W high pressure sodium lamp each. Some light spills from the storefronts onto portions of the sidewalk.

HPS/250W

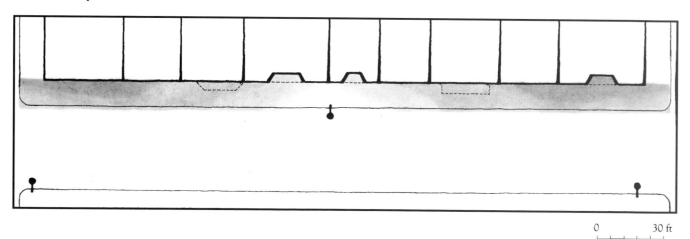

0   30 ft

Sense of Security	Appearance	Initial Equipment Cost	Annual Cost		Average Horizontal Illuminance	Connected Load
			Maintenance	Energy		
★★	★	—	—	—	0.78 fc	—

Upgrade

Twelve downlight wall luminaires and two HID downlights eliminate dark spaces between the street lights and under the overhangs. Seven downlight wall luminaires with 70-W high pressure sodium lamps are mounted below the 9 to 12-ft high retractable awnings. Five more downlight wall luminaires with 100-W high pressure sodium lamps are mounted 15-ft high on buildings without overhangs or awnings, providing light over an even greater part of the sidewalk. The ceiling of the 10-ft high overhang proves appropriate for the two recessed HID downlights, each with a 70-W high pressure sodium lamp. The shielding of the downlight wall luminaires limits light trespass into residences on the upper floors. The cobrahead street lights remain unchanged.

⬛ HPS/70,100W   • HPS/70W   ⬤ HPS/250W

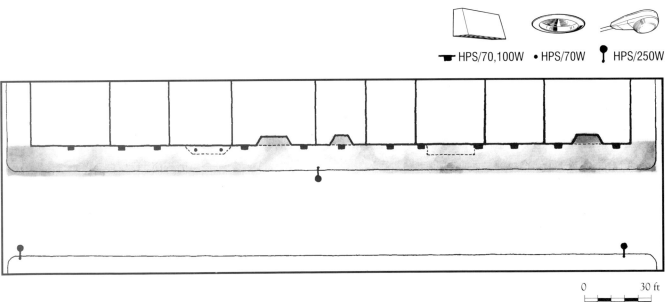

0   30 ft

Sense of Security	Appearance	Initial Equipment Cost	Annual Cost		Average Horizontal Illuminance	Connected Load
			Maintenance	Energy		
★★★★	★★★	$3000	$140	$660	5.8 fc	1500 W

Redesign 1

A unified shopping district design uses six performance post tops with 150-W high pressure sodium lamps mounted one each on 15-ft poles. These luminaires give a uniform look to this shopping area, while limiting glare on the street and light trespass into the residences on the upper floors. The cobrahead street lights remain unchanged.

Redesign 2

When 150-W metal halide lamps replace the high pressure sodium lamps in the six performance post tops, the shopping district appears more attractive because of the better color rendering property of metal halide lamps. The cobrahead street lights remain unchanged.

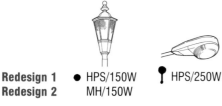

Redesign 1 ● HPS/150W ⅊ HPS/250W
Redesign 2 MH/150W

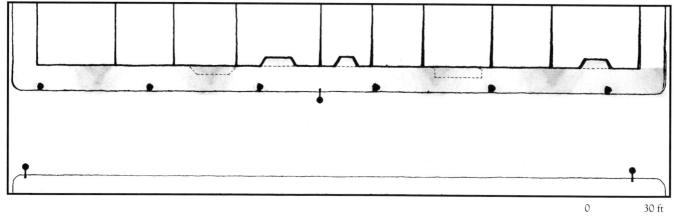

0   30 ft

	Sense of Security	Appearance	Initial Equipment Cost	Annual Cost		Average Horizontal Illuminance	Connected Load
				Maintenance	Energy		
Redesign 1	★★★★	★★★	$5000	$67	$490	2.2 fc	1100 W
Redesign 2	★★★★	★★★★	$5100	$130	$500	2.0 fc	1100 W

BUSINESS DISTRICT

*T**he business districts of many urban centers share a common look—wide sidewalks, trees, bus shelters, and recessed ground-level colonnades, all set amid a variety of buildings.*

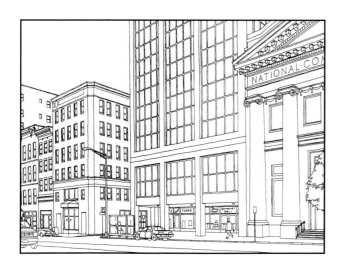

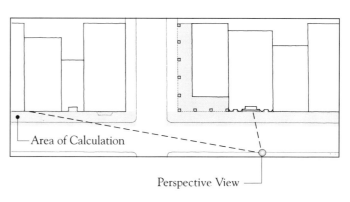

Area of Calculation

Perspective View

	Sense of Security	Appearance	Initial Equipment Cost	Annual Cost	
				Maintenance	Energy
Typical (p. 18)	★★	★★	—	$680	$460
Upgrade (p. 19)	★★★★	★★★	$5900	$280	$1300
Redesign (p. 20)	★★★★★	★★★★	$15,000	$370	$1100

Key: ★ Poorest ★★★★★ Best

Typical

Four 250-W high pressure sodium lamps, each mounted in a cobrahead on a 35-ft pole, provide street lighting. Seven recessed incandescent downlights, each housing a 150-W A-lamp, light the 15-ft high colonnade.

 HPS/250W    • INC/150W

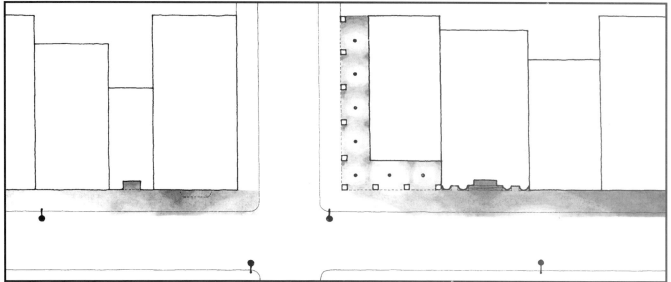

0   50 ft

Sense of Security	Appearance	Initial Equipment Cost	Annual Cost		Average Horizontal Illuminance	Connected Load
			Maintenance	Energy		
★★	★★	—	$680	$460	1.2 fc	1100 W

Upgrade

The ceiling of the colonnade houses seven canopy lights surface mounted over existing junction boxes. Each of the seven luminaires houses a 100-W metal halide lamp. Brackets hold 11 performance post tops, each housing a 150-W high pressure sodium lamp, 12-ft high on the walls. The cobra-head street lights remain unchanged.

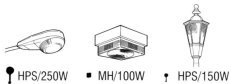

HPS/250W   ▪ MH/100W   HPS/150W

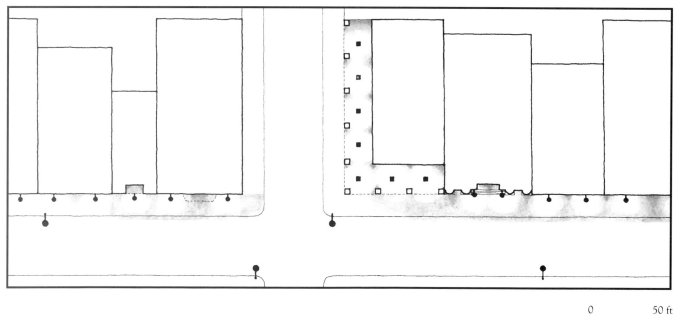

0   50 ft

Sense of Security	Appearance	Initial Equipment Cost	Annual Cost		Average Horizontal Illuminance	Connected Load
			Maintenance	Energy		
★★★★	★★★	$5900	$280	$1300	3.5 fc	2900 W

Redesign

A unified business district design utilizes nine decorative cutoffs mounted on 18-ft poles. Each decorative cutoff houses a 150-W metal halide lamp. Seven recessed HID downlights with 100-W metal halide lamps light the colonnade. Pruning the tree reduces shadows on the sidewalk. The cobrahead street lights remain unchanged.

 HPS/250W   ◆ MH/150W   • MH/100W

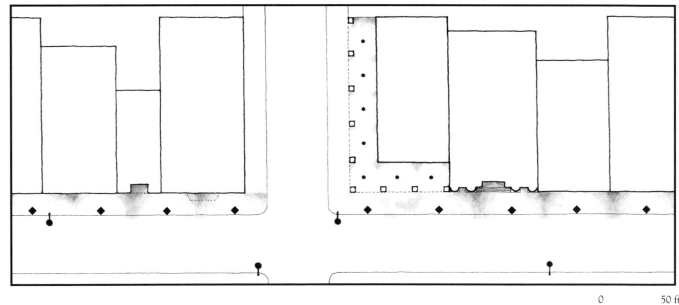

0   50 ft

Sense of Security	Appearance	Initial Equipment Cost	Annual Cost		Average Horizontal Illuminance	Connected Load
			Maintenance	Energy		
★★★★★	★★★★	$15,000	$370	$1100	3.9 fc	2600 W

PEDESTRIAN MALL

C ities and villages convert streets to pedestrian walkways as part of efforts to revitalize their business districts. People are attracted to the downtown by decorative pavings, plantings, lighting, and the vehicle-free atmosphere.

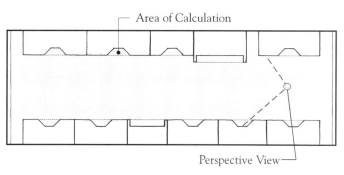

Area of Calculation

Perspective View

	Sense of Security	Appearance	Initial Equipment Cost	Annual Cost	
				Maintenance	Energy
Typical (p. 22)	★★	★★★	—	$1200	$790
Upgrade (p. 23)	★★★★	★★★	$3700	$270	$660
Redesign (p. 24)	★★★★★	★★★★	$17,000	$310	$660
Controls Option (p. 25)	—	—	$17,000	$230	$490

Key: ★ Poorest ★★★★★ Best

Typical

Twelve decorative post tops with 150-W incandescent A-lamps are mounted on two rows of 10-ft poles. These plain luminaires, often called "lollipops," cause glare and add little style to the mall. Passersby sometimes feel uncomfortable at night when some of the businesses are closed and their recessed entrances go dark.

● INC/150W

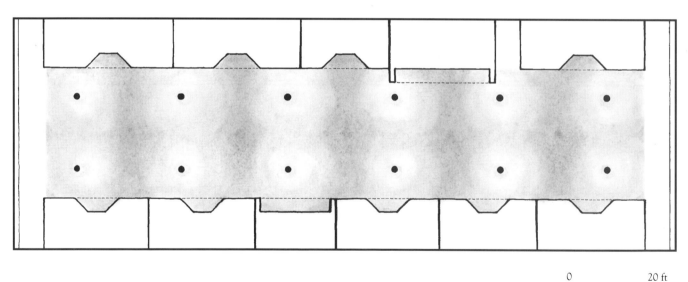

0   20 ft

Sense of Security	Appearance	Initial Equipment Cost	Annual Cost		Average Horizontal Illuminance	Connected Load
			Maintenance	Energy		
★★	★★★	—	$1200	$790	0.43 fc	1800 W

Upgrade

Twelve performance post tops with 100-W metal halide lamps replace the existing luminaires on poles that have been extended to 12-ft. The increased pole height allows the new luminaires to brighten the mall and introduce light to the entrance recesses while controlling glare and reducing operating costs.

● MH/100W

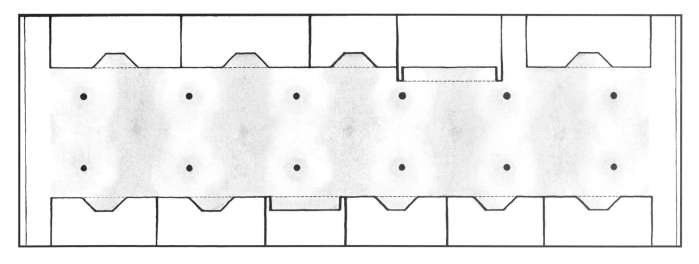

0   20 ft

Sense of Security	Appearance	Initial Equipment Cost	Annual Cost		Average Horizontal Illuminance	Connected Load
			Maintenance	Energy		
★★★★	★★★	$3700	$270	$660	2.0 fc	1500 W

Redesign

Twelve decorative cutoffs housing 100-W metal halide lamps atop new 20-ft poles increase the light directed onto the walkway. The decorative cutoffs also complement the mall's architecture.

● MH/100W

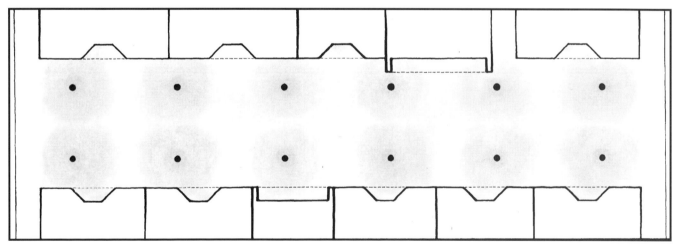

0   20 ft

Sense of Security	Appearance	Initial Equipment Cost	Annual Cost		Average Horizontal Illuminance	Connected Load
			Maintenance	Energy		
★★★★★	★★★★	$17,000	$310	$660	3.8 fc	1500 W

Controls Option

A time clock switches six alternating lamps off at midnight on one night and the other lamps the following night to save energy and maintain similar burning hours for all the lamps. Even after midnight, good uniformity and illuminance are maintained.

● MH/100W

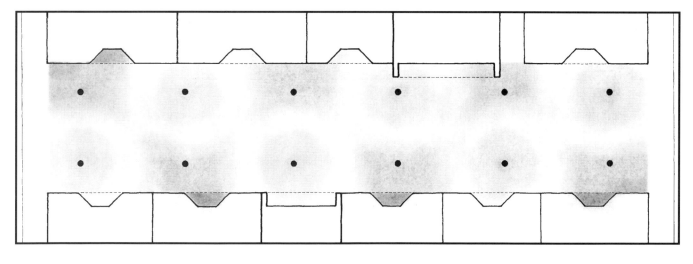

0   20 ft

| Sense of Security | Appearance | Initial Equipment Cost | Annual Cost | | Average Horizontal Illuminance | Connected Load |
			Maintenance	Energy		
—	—	$17,000	$230	$490	1.9 fc*	—

* Illuminance when time-clock switched luminaires are off.

QUICK STOP SHOPPING 1

Q uick Stop businesses rely on easy vehicular access for their customers. Customers park head-in at the curb or walk across the parking lot from the street. The sidewalk in front of the stores is not protected by an overhang.

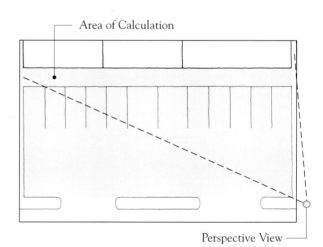

Area of Calculation

Perspective View

	Sense of Security	Appearance	Initial Equipment Cost	Annual Cost	
				Maintenance	Energy
Typical (p. 28)	★	★	—	$22	$170
Upgrade (p. 29)	★★★	★★	$3600	$65	$330
Redesign (p. 30)	★★★★	★★★★	$5500	$150	$680

Key: ★ Poorest   ★★★★★ Best

Typical

Although aimed toward the street, a cobrahead housing a 250-W high pressure sodium lamp provides some light in the parking lot. Wall packs on either end of the building each house a 150-W high pressure sodium lamp. The glare from the wall packs makes it difficult to see the stores, pedestrians, and other vehicles. Tripping on the curb is a hazard due to the dark areas on the sidewalk.

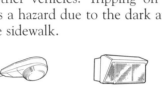

HPS/250W   HPS/150W

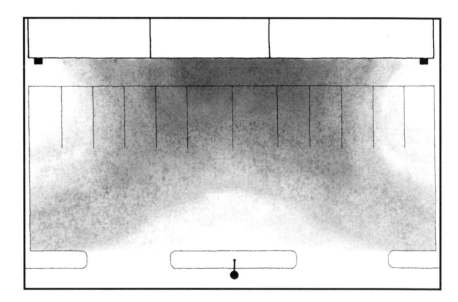

0   20 ft

Sense of Security	Appearance	Initial Equipment Cost	Annual Cost		Average Horizontal Illuminance	Connected Load
			Maintenance	Energy		
★	★	—	$22	$170	1.0 fc	380 W

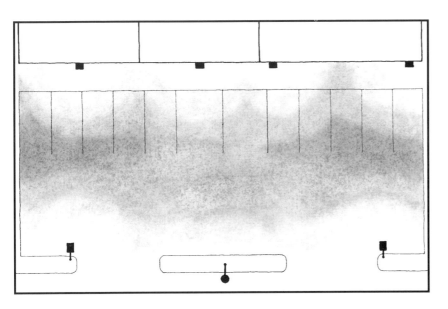

Upgrade

Four shielded wall packs with 70-W high pressure sodium lamps are mounted 11 or 14-ft high on the fascia. Two type III cutoffs with 150-W high pressure sodium lamps are mounted on the 25-ft poles at the entrance and exit. The cobrahead street light remains unchanged.

HPS/250W   HPS/70W   HPS/150W

0   20 ft

Sense of Security	Appearance	Initial Equipment Cost	Annual Cost		Average Horizontal Illuminance	Connected Load
			Maintenance	Energy		
★★★	★★	$3600	$65	$330	2.0 fc	760 W

Redesign

Thirteen fluorescent sign lighters, mounted 12 and 15-ft high, light the building facade, the signs, the sidewalk, and front of the parking lot. The sign lighters each contain an 8-ft 75-W slimline T12 RE741 lamp with electronic ballasts. Two type III cutoffs with 150-W high pressure sodium lamps on 25-ft poles light the rest of the parking lot. The cobrahead street light remains unchanged.

HPS/250W   FL/75W T12   HPS/150W

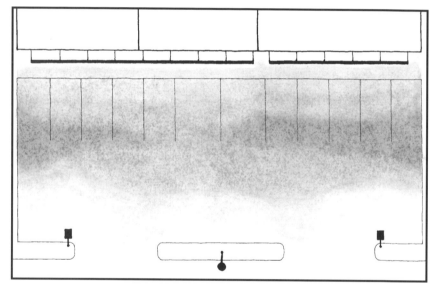

0   20 ft

Sense of Security	Appearance	Initial Equipment Cost	Annual Cost		Average Horizontal Illuminance	Connected Load
			Maintenance	Energy		
★★★★	★★★★	$5500	$150	$680	4.0 fc	1500 W

QUICK STOP SHOPPING 2

C ustomers park their cars head in and make quick purchases at these small businesses. A 10-ft high overhang shelters the sidewalk in front of the entrances.

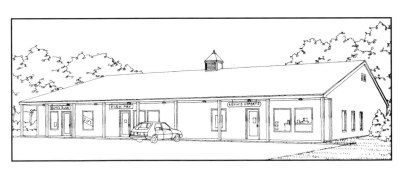

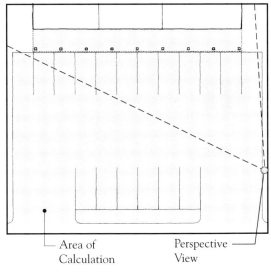

Area of Calculation

Perspective View

	Sense of Security	Appearance	Initial Equipment Cost	Annual Cost	
				Maintenance	Energy
Typical (p. 32)	★	★★	—	$740	$440
Upgrade (p. 33)	★★★	★★★	$1200	$98	$240
Redesign (p. 34)	★★★★	★★★★	$4100	$88	$460
Controls Option (p. 34)	—	—	$4100	$50	$250

Key: ★ Poorest ★★★★★ Best

Typical

A single flood light with a 175-W mercury vapor lamp on a 20-ft pole lights only the center of the parking lot and creates glare for customers leaving the stores or driving away. Eight incandescent downlights with 100-W A lamps light the sidewalk, but must be replaced often. The signs are difficult to see.

- INC/100W   ▪ MV/175W

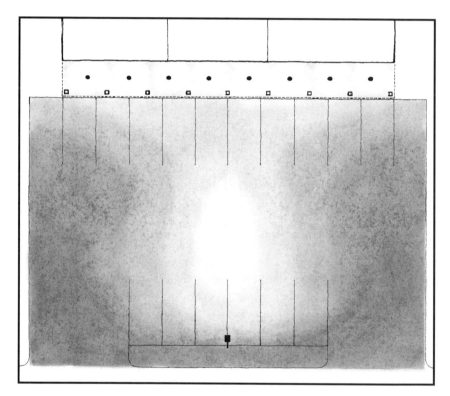

0   20 ft

Sense of Security	Appearance	Initial Equipment Cost	Annual Cost		Average Horizontal Illuminance	Connected Load
			Maintenance	Energy		
★	★★	—	$740	$440	0.35 fc*	1000 W

* Illuminance under the canopy is 1.6 fc.

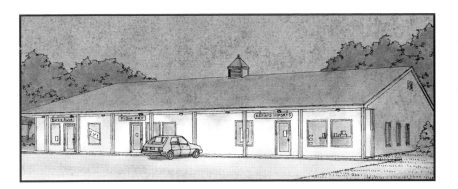

Upgrade

The flood light is replaced by a type III cutoff with a 250-W high pressure sodium lamp mounted on a 30-ft pole. The luminaire's light distribution and higher mounting improves the uniformity in the parking lot and reduces glare. Eight performance versions of the decorative surface luminaire mounted under the overhang, each with a 28-W compact fluorescent lamp, reduce operating costs.

• CFL/28W   HPS/250W

0   20 ft

Sense of Security	Appearance	Initial Equipment Cost	Annual Cost		Average Horizontal Illuminance	Connected Load
			Maintenance	Energy		
★★★	★★★	$1200	$98	$240	1.6 fc*	560 W

* Illuminance under the canopy is 2.0 fc.

Redesign

Two type III cutoffs with 250-W metal halide lamps, each atop a 30-ft pole, provide good uniformity, color, and glare control for the parking lot. Four enclosed fluorescent strip luminaires with 8-ft 75-W slimline T12 RE741 fluorescent lamps mounted under the overhang light the sidewalk. Three additional enclosed fluorescent luminaires with 4-ft 32-W T8 fluorescent lamps are mounted behind the fascia in front of the signs, greatly improving their visibility.

Controls Option

At midnight, a time clock turns off all but the sign lights because the stores have closed and security is not a major concern to these businesses. The time clock reduces operating costs. Passersby see the signs clearly, but the parking lot is very dark.

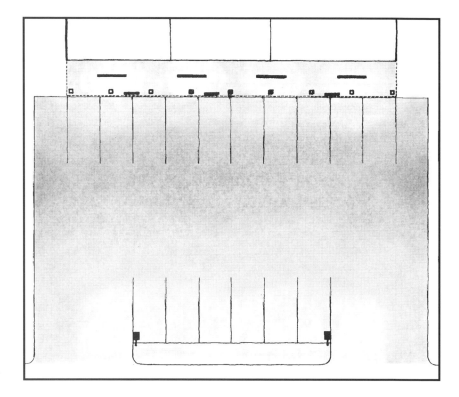

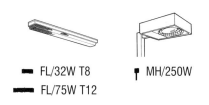

- FL/32W T8
- FL/75W T12

⎸ MH/250W

0   20 ft

	Sense of Security	Appearance	Initial Equipment Cost	Annual Cost		Average Horizontal Illuminance	Connected Load
				Maintenance	Energy		
Redesign	★★★★	★★★★	$4100	$88	$460	1.8 fc*	1100 W
Controls Option	—	—	$4100	$50	$250	0.18 fc**	—

* Illuminance under the canopy is 6.3 fc.
** Illuminance when time-clock switched luminaires are off. Illuminance under the canopy is 1.4 fc.

LOCAL SHOPPING CENTER

A covered walkway between the 24-hr local supermarket and the discount department store provides shelter for customers walking from one store to another. The customers arrive by car and walk through the large parking lot.

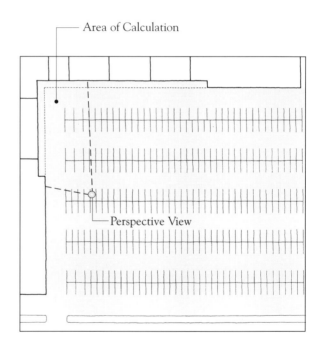

Area of Calculation

Perspective View

	Sense of Security	Appearance	Initial Equipment Cost	Annual Cost	
				Maintenance	Energy
Typical (p. 36)	★★★	★	—	$200	$2900
Upgrade (p. 37)	★★★	★★★	$5200	$260	$3000
Redesign (p. 38)	★★★★★	★★★★	$35,000	$940	$6700
Controls Option (p. 39)	—	—	$35,000	$840	$5500

Key: ★ Poorest   ★★★★★ Best

Typical

Twelve cobraheads with 400-W clear mercury vapor lamps mounted back to back on six 35-ft poles light the parking lot. Thirteen open fluorescent strips with 8-ft 75-W cool-white T12 slimline lamps are spaced 25-ft apart on the ceiling of the 15-ft high ceiling of the walkway. These inexpensive luminaires do little to control glare, and the mercury vapor lamps are poor color sources.

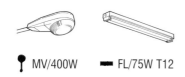

MV/400W   FL/75W T12

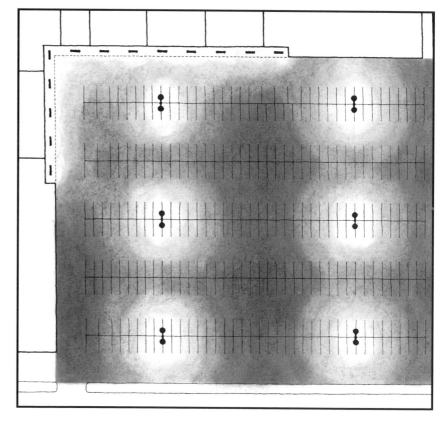

0   75 ft

Sense of Security	Appearance	Initial Equipment Cost	Annual Cost		Average Horizontal Illuminance	Connected Load
			Maintenance	Energy		
★★★	★	—	$200	$2900	1.2 fc*	6600 W

* Illuminance on the sidewalk is 5.3 fc.

Upgrade

Twelve type III cutoffs replace the cobraheads on the six existing 35-ft poles, providing better glare control. Twelve 400-W high pressure sodium lamps replace the mercury vapor lamps, providing improved color. Thirteen 8-ft 75-W slimline T12 RE741 fluorescent lamps with low-temperature ballasts replace the cool-white lamps along the walkway. In cold climates, 8-ft high-output lamps may prove more suitable.

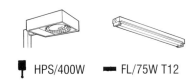

■ HPS/400W   ▬ FL/75W T12

0   75 ft

Sense of Security	Appearance	Initial Equipment Cost	Annual Cost		Average Horizontal Illuminance	Connected Load
			Maintenance	Energy		
★★★	★★★	$5200	$260	$3000	2.6 fc*	6700 W

* Illuminance on the sidewalk is 5.4 fc.

Redesign

Twelve type V cutoffs, mounted one to a 40-ft pole, each house a 1000-W metal halide lamp, lighting the parking lot uniformly. Light from nineteen 100-W metal halide lamps, each in a canopy light, brightens the walkway.

■ MH/1000W   ▪ MH/100W

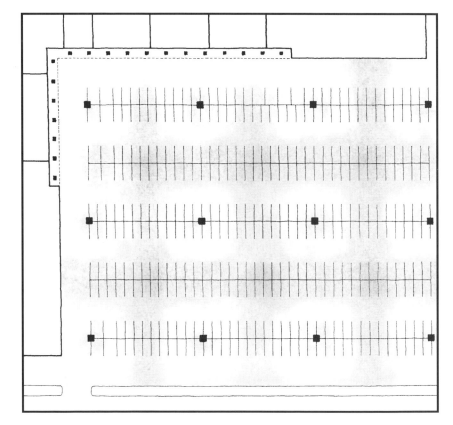

0   75 ft

Sense of Security	Appearance	Initial Equipment Cost	Annual Cost		Average Horizontal Illuminance	Connected Load
			Maintenance	Energy		
★★★★★	★★★★	$35,000	$940	$6700	3.7 fc*	15,000 W

* Illuminance on the sidewalk is 8.3 fc.

Controls Option

A time clock switches off five of the 12 type V cutoffs at 11:00 p.m., reducing the cost of operating the lighting system. The luminaires near the 24-hour supermarket are left on all night for the safety of customers who park nearby. Some dark areas result, which may reduce the sense of security in the parking lot late at night.

■ MH/1000W   ▪ MH/100W

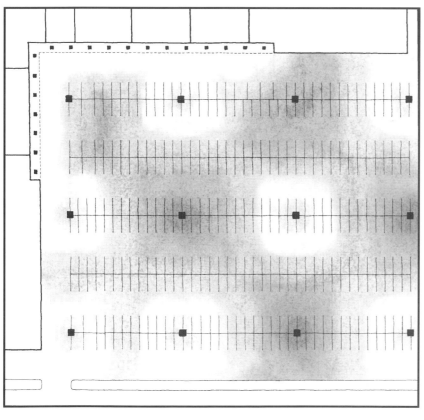

0   75 ft

Sense of Security	Appearance	Initial Equipment Cost	Annual Cost		Average Horizontal Illuminance	Connected Load
			Maintenance	Energy		
—	—	$35,000	$840	$5500	2.5 fc*	—

* Illuminance when time-clock switched luminaires are off. Illuminance on the sidewalk is 6.9 fc.

OFFICE PARK

*T*he suburban office park often includes ample parking, lawns, and wooded borders.

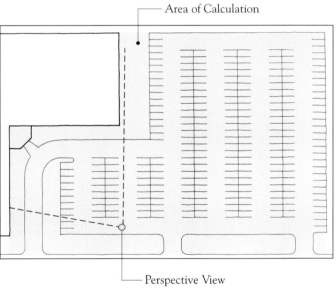

Area of Calculation

Perspective View

	Sense of Security	Appearance	Initial Equipment Cost	Annual Cost	
				Maintenance	Energy
Typical (p. 42)	★★	★	—	$450	$2200
Upgrade (p. 43)	★★★	★★★	$13,000	$410	$2500
Redesign (p. 44)	★★★	★★★★	$24,000	$380	$2800

Key: ★ Poorest ★★★★★ Best

Typical

The parking lot's five 30-ft poles, with two flood lights each, provide locations for ten 250-W high pressure sodium lamps. Mounted 23-ft high on the walls, four halogen flood lights with 500-W tubular halogen lamps only partially light the front of the building, leaving large dark areas. Glare poses a problem for both drivers and pedestrians. Two decorative surface luminaires with 60-W A-lamps mark the entry.

⬥ HPS/250W   ▼ TH/500W   • INC/60W

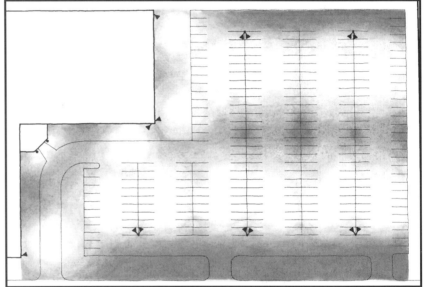

0   75 ft

Sense of Security	Appearance	Initial Equipment Cost	Annual Cost		Average Horizontal Illuminance	Connected Load
			Maintenance	Energy		
★★	★	—	$450	$2200	0.96 fc	5100 W

Upgrade

Three additional 30-ft poles provide more positions for mounting luminaires. Two type III cutoffs with 250-W high pressure sodium lamps, mounted back to back on each of the eight poles, distribute light evenly over the parking lot. Six type III cutoffs with 100-W metal halide lamps mounted 25-ft high on the building light the walk and complement the blue-gray split-block facade. A 23-W screwbase compact fluorescent lamp replaces the incandescent lamp in each of the decorative surface luminaires at the entry.

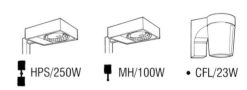

| ■ HPS/250W | ■ MH/100W | • CFL/23W |

0   75 ft

Sense of Security	Appearance	Initial Equipment Cost	Annual Cost		Average Horizontal Illuminance	Connected Load
			Maintenance	Energy		
★★★	★★★	$13,000	$410	$2500	1.7 fc	5600 W

Redesign

Eight new 35-ft poles in the parking lot provide mounting locations for 11 type III cutoffs with a 400-W metal halide lamp. Around the perimeter of the lot, the luminaires are mounted one per pole. The three poles near the center each support two luminaires mounted back to back. From atop 10-ft poles, ten performance post tops with 100-W metal halide lamps light the walk and complement the color of the grass and trees.

 MH/400W   MH/100W

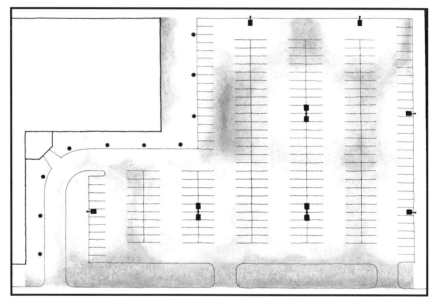

0   75 ft

Sense of Security	Appearance	Initial Equipment Cost	Annual Cost		Average Horizontal Illuminance	Connected Load
			Maintenance	Energy		
★★★	★★★★	$24,000	$380	$2800	1.7 fc	6300 W

PARKING STRUCTURE 1

*S*hoppers, some laden with packages, may struggle to remember where they parked their cars in this multi-story garage. Others may hurry past the many hiding places directly towards their cars, worrying that their cars have been burglarized or vandalized. The 9-ft high ceiling is a flat concrete slab that spans the deep structural beams.

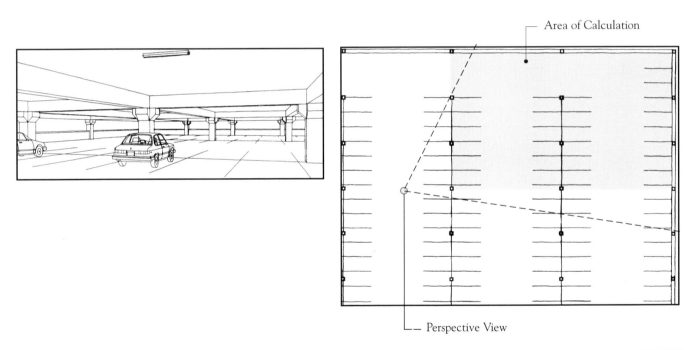

Area of Calculation

Perspective View

	Sense of Security	Appearance	Initial Equipment Cost	Annual Cost	
				Maintenance	Energy
Typical (p. 46)	★★	★★	—	$33	$240
Upgrade (p. 47)	★★★	★★	$230	$76	$480
Redesign 1 (p. 48)	★★★	★★★	$1200	$200	$720
Redesign 2 (p. 49)	★★★★	★★★★	$3600	$550	$1300
Redesign 3 (p. 50)	★★★★★	★★★	$3500	$250	$1400

Key: ★ Poorest   ★★★★★ Best

Typical

Six open fluorescent strips with 4-ft 40-W T12 cool-white lamps are mounted in the center of each structural bay. Spill light from the adjacent bays does not eliminate the shadows between the cars. Glare distracts and tends to blind drivers. High car antennas and vandals often break the unenclosed and unprotected lamps,. A single broken lamp can make an entire bay very dark.

FL/40W T12

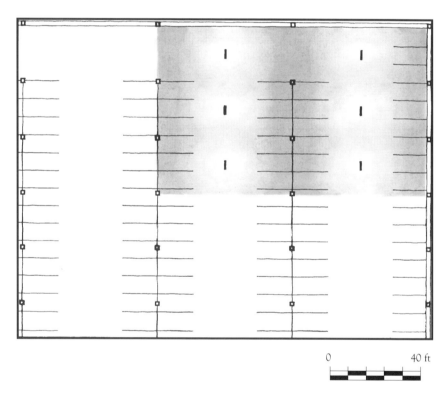

0   40 ft

Sense of Security	Appearance	Initial Equipment Cost	Annual Cost		Average Horizontal Illuminance	Connected Load
			Maintenance	Energy		
★★	★★	—	$33	$240	0.93 fc	280 W

Upgrade

Surface raceway wiring allows the garage operators to reposition the six existing open fluorescent strips and add six new open fluorescent strips to provide more-uniform light distribution from ceiling-mounting positions above the bumpers of the parked cars. The open fluorescent strips each house one 4-ft 40-W T-12 RE741 lamp, which meets the requirements of the 1992 Energy Policy Act. The same act eliminates the 4-ft 40-W T12 cool-white and many other lamps from the United States market.

■ FL/40W T12

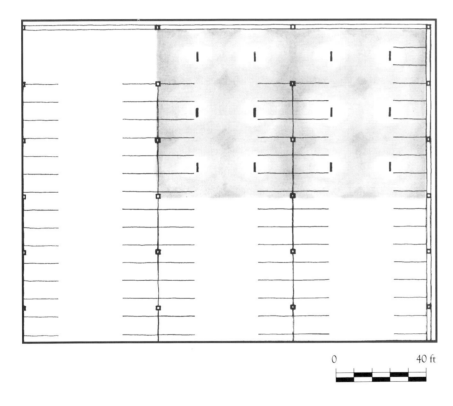

0   40 ft

Sense of Security	Appearance	Initial Equipment Cost	Annual Cost		Average Horizontal Illuminance	Connected Load
			Maintenance	Energy		
★★★	★★	$230	$76	$480	1.9 fc	550 W

Redesign 1

Twelve ceiling-mounted enclosed fluorescent strips, each with two 4-ft 32-W T8 RE741 fluorescent lamps, provide better light levels and good distribution. The enclosed luminaire protects the lamps and improves their ability to start in cold weather. A low-temperature ballast should also be considered.

FL/32W T8

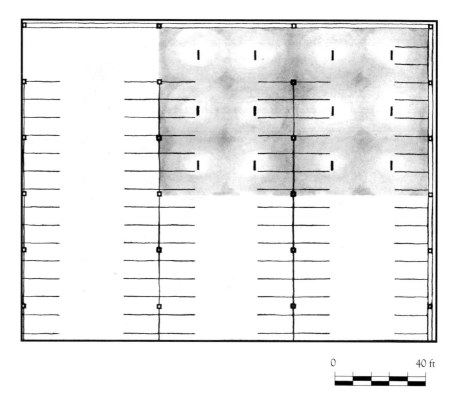

0   40 ft

Sense of Security	Appearance	Initial Equipment Cost	Annual Cost		Average Horizontal Illuminance	Connected Load
			Maintenance	Energy		
★★★	★★★	$1200	$200	$720	3.0 fc	820 W

Redesign 2

Twelve shielded garage luminaires with 100-W metal halide lamps provide good color and uniformity and high light levels.

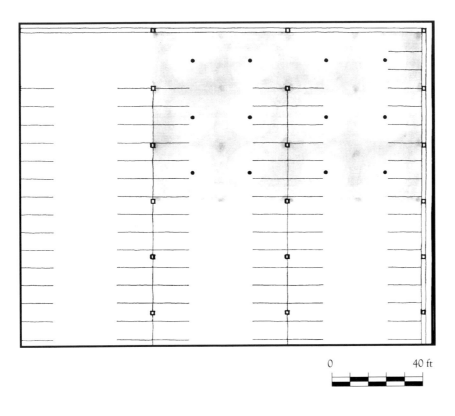

0   40 ft

● MH/100W

Sense of Security	Appearance	Initial Equipment Cost	Annual Cost		Average Horizontal Illuminance	Connected Load
			Maintenance	Energy		
★★★★	★★★★	$3600	$550	$1300	4.1 fc	1500 W

Redesign 3

Twelve shielded garage luminaires with 100-W high pressure sodium lamps provide light levels and uniformity that meet IESNA standards for parking facilities.

● HPS/100W

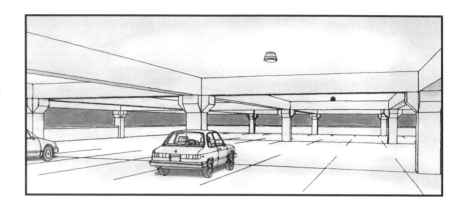

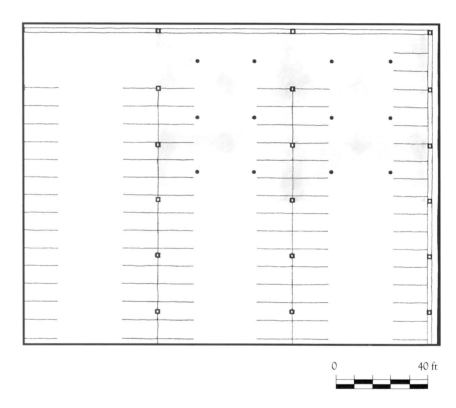

0   40 ft

Sense of Security	Appearance	Initial Equipment Cost	Annual Cost		Average Horizontal Illuminance	Connected Load
			Maintenance	Energy		
★★★★★	★★★	$3500	$250	$1400	5.2 fc	1600 W

PARKING STRUCTURE 2

C ar owners, some laden with packages, may struggle to remember where they parked in this underground lot. Others may hurry past the many hiding places towards their parking spaces, worrying about their safety or that their cars have been burglarized or vandalized. The garage has 8-ft clearance below its waffle-slab concrete ceiling.

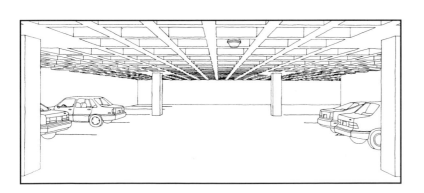

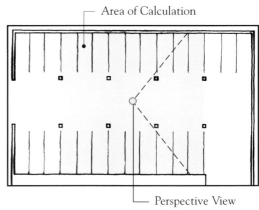

Area of Calculation

Perspective View

	Sense of Security	Appearance	Initial Equipment Cost	Annual Cost	
				Maintenance	Energy
Typical (p. 52)	★★	★	—	$42	$230
Redesign 1 (p. 53)	★★★	★★	$230	$76	$480
Redesign 2 (p. 54)	★★★★	★★★	$3000	$76	$480
Redesign 3 (p. 55)	★★★★	★★★	$860	$110	$950
Redesign 4 (p. 56)	★★★★	★★★	$2100	$270	$2000
Redesign 5 (p. 56)	★★★★	★★★★	$2200	$510	$2000

Key: ★ Poorest ★★★★★ Best

Typical

Two refractor baskets with 100-W high pressure sodium lamps centered over the driving lane provide general illumination. However, if either of these lamps burn out or is vandalized, a large area is left dark. The waffled coffer absorbs much of the light, especially if the luminaires are mounted too deep in the coffers. Lowering the luminaire reduces vehicle clearance and creates glare. The dark walls contribute to the gloomy atmosphere.

● HPS/100W

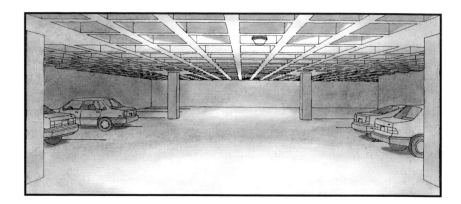

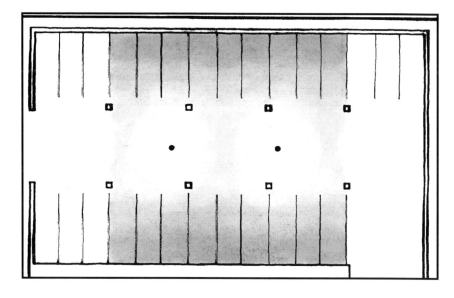

0   25 ft

Sense of Security	Appearance	Initial Equipment Cost	Annual Cost		Average Horizontal Illuminance	Connected Load
			Maintenance	Energy		
★★	★	—	$42	$230	1.6 fc	260 W

Redesign 1

Six open fluorescent strips mounted over the edges of the driving lane improve uniformity and brighten the walls. The six luminaires each house two 4-ft 40-W T12 RE741 fluorescent lamps.

■ FL/40W T12

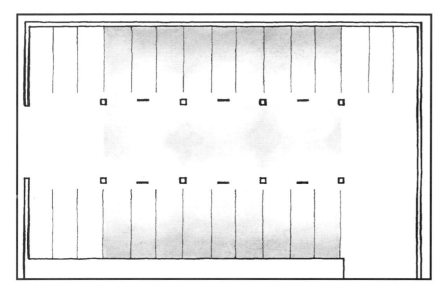

0   25 ft

Sense of Security	Appearance	Initial Equipment Cost	Annual Cost		Average Horizontal Illuminance	Connected Load
			Maintenance	Energy		
★★★	★★	$230	$76	$480	2.9 fc	550 W

Redesign 2

Six open fluorescent strips, each with two 4-ft 40-W T12 RE741 fluorescent lamps, are mounted over the edges of the driving lane. White paint on the concrete ceiling and walls increases the reflectance of these surfaces, raising the average horizontal illuminance and adding to the feeling of brightness in the garage.

— FL/40W T12

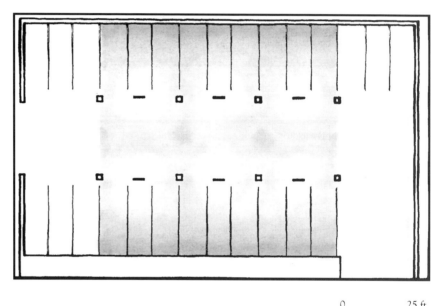

0   25 ft

Sense of Security	Appearance	Initial Equipment Cost	Annual Cost		Average Horizontal Illuminance	Connected Load
			Maintenance	Energy		
★★★★	★★★	$3000	$76*	$480	4.4 fc	550 W

* Does not include painting.

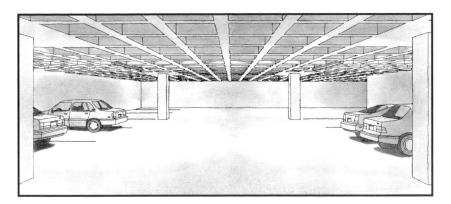

Redesign 3

Six enclosed fluorescent strips are mounted over the edges of the driving lane. Each has two 8-ft 75-W slimline T12 RE741 fluorescent lamps, giving high illuminance and good uniformity.

▬ FL/75W T12

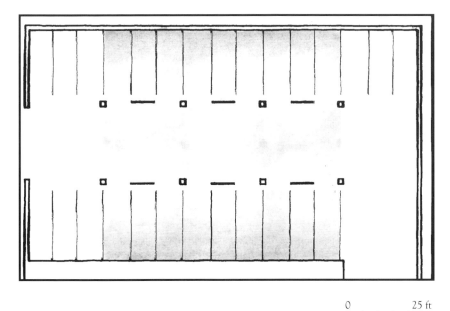

0   25 ft

Sense of Security	Appearance	Initial Equipment Cost	Annual Cost		Average Horizontal Illuminance	Connected Load
			Maintenance	Energy		
★★★★	★★★	$860	$110	$950	5.2 fc	1100 W

Redesign 4

Six shielded garage luminaires with 150-W high pressure sodium lamps are mounted over the edges of the driving lane. The shielded luminaires reduce glare and improve uniformity.

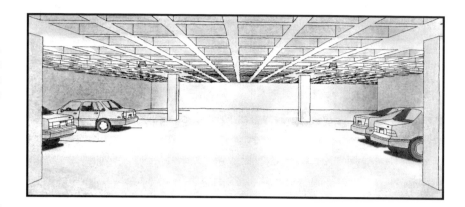

Redesign 5

The six shielded garage luminaires with 150-W metal halide lamps provide better color but reduced illumination.

Redesign 4 • HPS/150W
Redesign 5   MH/150W

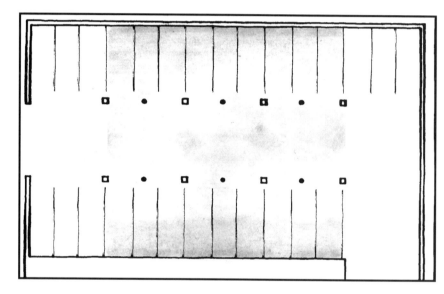

0   25 ft

	Sense of Security	Appearance	Initial Equipment Cost	Annual Cost		Average Horizontal Illuminance	Connected Load
				Maintenance	Energy		
Redesign 4	★★★★	★★★	$2100	$270	$2000	6.8 fc	2300 W
Redesign 5	★★★★	★★★★	$2200	$510	$2000	5.0 fc	2300 W

AUTO DEALER

*A*uto dealers hope that drivers will be attracted to the new cars parked along the busy retail strip. Even in the evening, customers walk the lot, looking at the styling, features, and stickers of the cars. Service customers sometimes drop off their cars before the dealership opens, and occasionally leave them overnight.

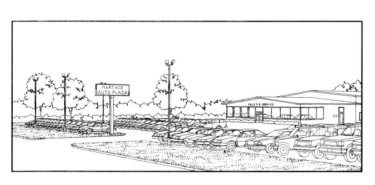

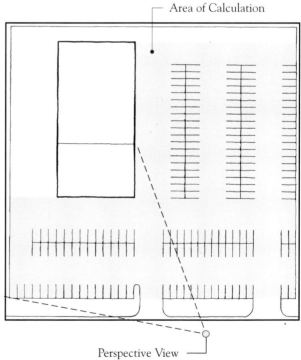

Area of Calculation

Perspective View

	Sense of Security	Appearance	Initial Equipment Cost	Annual Cost	
				Maintenance	Energy
Typical (p. 58)	★★	★	—	$100	$2800
Upgrade (p. 59)	★★★	★★	$12,000	$310	$4800
Redesign 1 (p. 60)	★★★	★★★	$21,000	$540	$6300
Redesign 2 (p. 61)	★★★★	★★★	$26,000	$510	$6200

Key: ★ Poorest   ★★★★★ Best

Typical

Seven 25-ft poles positioned around the perimeter of the lot provide mounting positions for 14 flood lights, each with a 400-W mercury vapor lamp. The 14 luminaires do not provide enough light on the front row to make the cars stand out against other distractions or adequately light the parking spaces for service customers. A luminaire on one pole faces directly into traffic, causing a glare problem for drivers. The mercury lamps distort some colors, making the cars less attractive.

MV/400W

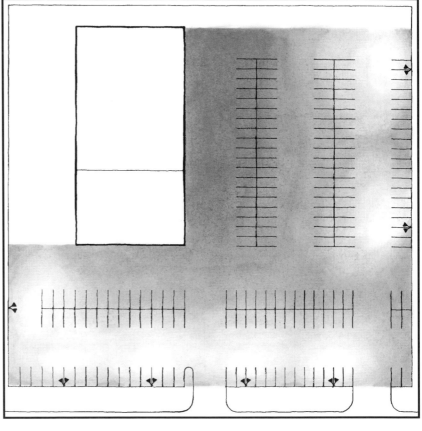

0   75 ft

Sense of Security	Appearance	Initial Equipment Cost	Annual Cost		Average Horizontal Illuminance	Connected Load
			Maintenance	Energy		
★★	★	—	$100	$2800	0.81 fc	6400 W

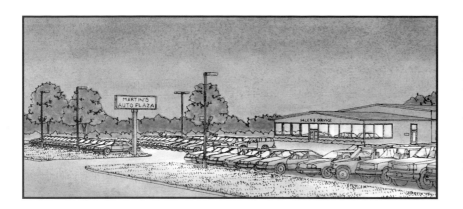

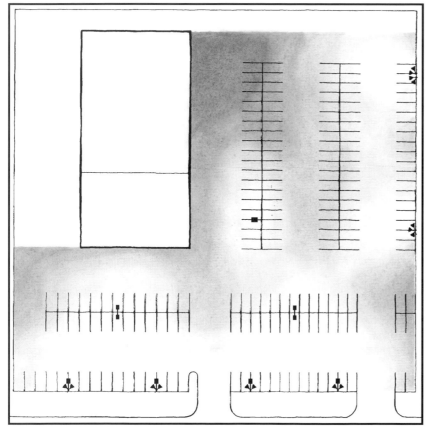

Upgrade

Six of the existing 25-ft poles on the perimeter of the lot provide mounting positions for new luminaires; one pole has been removed to eliminate the glare problem. The four existing poles along the road provide mounting positions for two flood lights and a type III cutoff, each housing a 400-W metal halide lamp, which increases curb appeal with higher light levels and better color. The other two existing poles provide mounting positions for flood lights, four on one pole, three on the other, each housing a 400-W metal halide lamp. Five additional type III cutoffs with 400-W metal halide lamps provide light and improve uniformity from atop three new poles within the lot. All the luminaires are mounted 25-ft high, except the eight flood lights on the poles along the roadway, which are mounted 12-ft high.

◢▶ MH/400W   ▮ MH/400 W

0   75 ft

Sense of Security	Appearance	Initial Equipment Cost	Annual Cost		Average Horizontal Illuminance	Connected Load
			Maintenance	Energy		
★★★	★★	$12,000	$310	$4800	2.6 fc	11,000 W

Redesign 1

To further improve curb appeal and increase illuminance on the cars, ten forward-throw type III cutoffs with 1000-W metal halide lamps are mounted on seven 25-ft poles at the front of the lot. Eight type III cutoffs with 400-W metal halide lamps, mounted in pairs on 35-ft poles, light the rest of the lot.

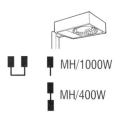

MH/1000W

MH/400W

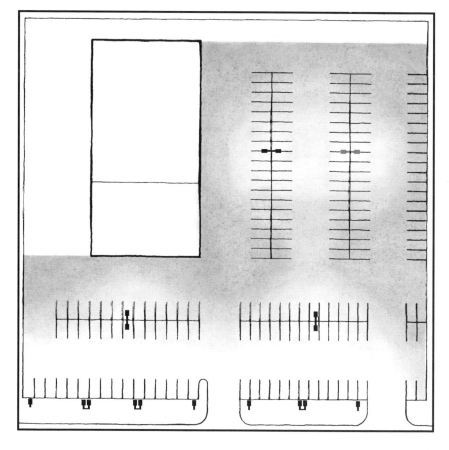

0   75 ft

Sense of Security	Appearance	Initial Equipment Cost	Annual Cost		Average Horizontal Illuminance	Connected Load
			Maintenance	Energy		
★★★	★★★	$21,000	$540	$6300	3.7 fc	14,000 W

Redesign 2

Eight forward-throw type III cutoffs with 1000-W metal halide lamps are mounted on eight 25-ft poles at the front of the lot. Twelve type III cutoffs with 400-W metal halide lamps, mounted in pairs on 35-ft poles, improve the uniformity of the lot.

█ MH/1000W

█ MH/400W

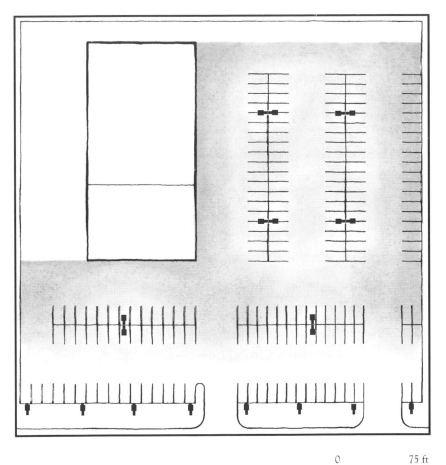

0   75 ft

Sense of Security	Appearance	Initial Equipment Cost	Annual Cost		Average Horizontal Illuminance	Connected Load
			Maintenance	Energy		
★★★★	★★★	$26,000	$510	$6200	3.7 fc	14,000 W

LOADING DOCK 1

*T*he deliveries received by many stores and smaller factories are unloaded on simple one- or two-bay loading docks, which are often located at the back of the building, near a rear entrance.

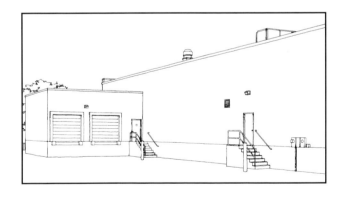

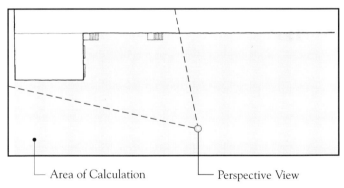

Area of Calculation — Perspective View

	Sense of Security	Appearance	Initial Equipment Cost	Annual Cost	
				Maintenance	Energy
Typical (p. 64)	★★	★	—	$45	$330
Upgrade (p. 65)	★★★	★★★	$1500	$79	$330
Redesign (p. 66)	★★★★	★★★	$3700	$94	$440

Key: ★ Poorest ★★★★★ Best

Typical

Four wall packs with 150-W high pressure sodium lamps are mounted 15-ft high on the walls, above truck height. Glare from the wall packs makes it difficult for drivers to see passersby and back their trucks into position. In smaller areas, wall packs will throw unwanted light onto neighboring properties.

HPS/150W

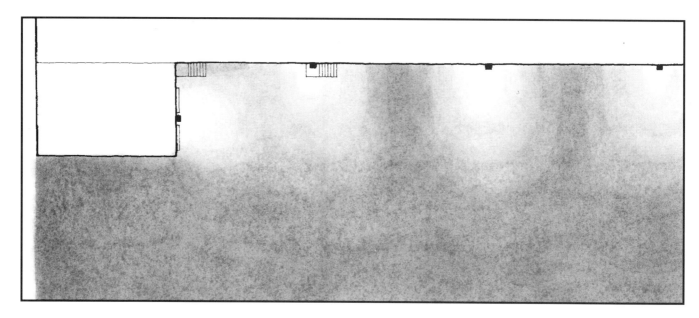

0   25 ft

Sense of Security	Appearance	Initial Equipment Cost	Annual Cost		Average Horizontal Illuminance	Connected Load
			Maintenance	Energy		
★★	★	—	$45	$330	0.99 fc	750 W

Upgrade

Eight front-shielded wall packs, mounted 15-ft high in four new locations on the wall and in the four existing locations, provide adequate light along the building's perimeter and create less glare than the wall packs. Each front-shielded wall pack houses a 70-W high pressure sodium lamp.

HPS/70W

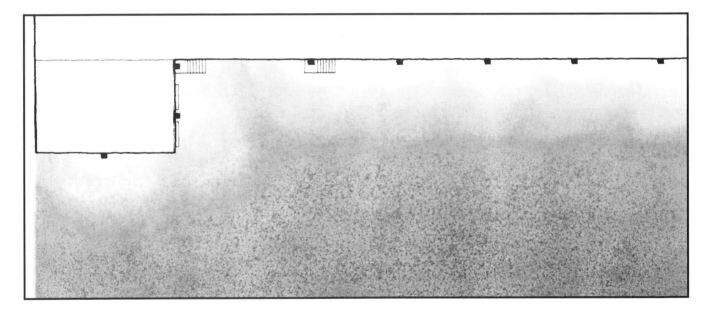

0   25 ft

Sense of Security	Appearance	Initial Equipment Cost	Annual Cost		Average Horizontal Illuminance	Connected Load
			Maintenance	Energy		
★★★	★★★	$1500	$79	$330	0.65 fc	760 W

Redesign

Five type III cutoffs with 100-W high pressure sodium lamps light the loading dock from locations 15-ft high on the building. Two more type III cutoffs with 100-W HPS lamps mounted on 20-ft poles increase coverage of the site. The cutoff luminaires shield a security camera, which has been mounted atop the pole, from the glare. A front-shielded wall pack with a 70-W high pressure sodium lamp mounted 15-ft high above the door lights the stairs near the loading bays, even when a truck blocks light from the other luminaires.

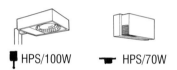

HPS/100W   HPS/70W

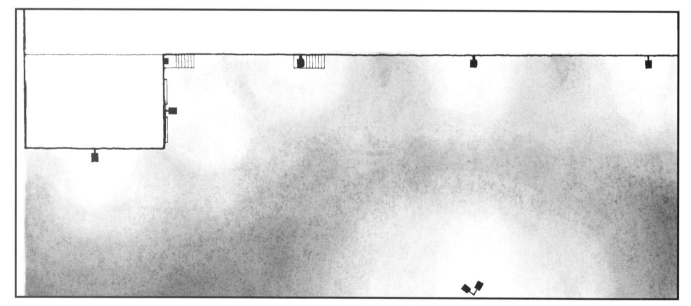

0   25 ft

Sense of Security	Appearance	Initial Equipment Cost	Annual Cost		Average Horizontal Illuminance	Connected Load
			Maintenance	Energy		
★★★★	★★★	$3700	$94	$440	1.3 fc	1000 W

LOADING DOCK 2

*O*ften, there will appear to be no space between the trucks backed up against the overhead doors of freight terminals and factories. A 15-ft high canopy provides some shelter for workers unloading pallets of often valuable goods. Sometimes the goods are stored temporarily inside the doors, making security an issue. During the summer, workers sometimes open the doors for relief from the heat.

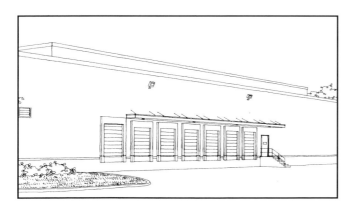

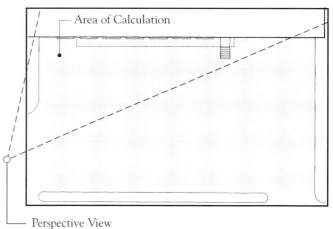

Area of Calculation

Perspective View

	Sense of Security	Appearance	Initial Equipment Cost	Annual Cost	
				Maintenance	Energy
Typical (p. 68)	★	★★	—	$280	$340
Upgrade (p. 69)	★★★	★★★	$1400	$60	$480
Redesign (p. 70)	★★★★★	★★★★	$4700	$89	$650

Key: ★ Poorest   ★★★★★ Best

Typical

A truck backed up to the loading dock can create a shadow by blocking the light from one of the four incandescent downlights with 150-W A-lamps recessed in the canopy. No light from these luminaires reaches spaces between trucks parked side by side. Two flood lights with 150-W high pressure sodium lamps mounted 25-ft high on the wall light the yard. Glare from these flood lights make the driver's job of backing up a truck to the loading bay difficult.

• INC/150W   HPS/150W

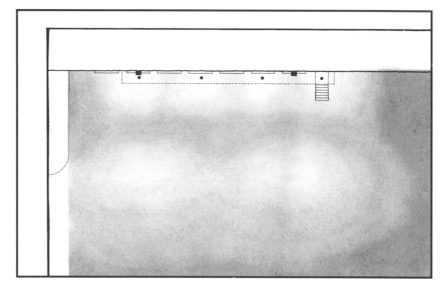

0   25 ft

Sense of Security	Appearance	Initial Equipment Cost	Annual Cost		Average Horizontal Illuminance	Connected Load
			Maintenance	Energy		
★	★★	—	$280	$340	0.57 fc	980 W

Upgrade

Under the canopy, six enclosed fluorescent strips with 8-ft 75-W slimline T12 RE741 fluorescent lamps light between trucks from positions between the overhead doors. Three performance wall packs with 150-W high pressure sodium lamps replace the flood lights, improving the uniformity of light in the lot and reducing glare.

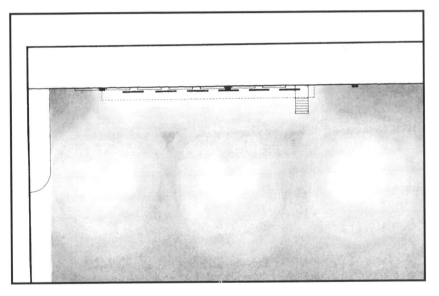

FL/75W T12   HPS/150W

0   25 ft

Sense of Security	Appearance	Initial Equipment Cost	Annual Cost		Average Horizontal Illuminance	Connected Load
			Maintenance	Energy		
★★★	★★★	$1400	$60	$480	1.4 fc	1100 W

Redesign

Under the canopy, six enclosed fluorescent strips with 8-ft 75-W slimline T12 RE741 fluorescent lamps light between the trucks from positions between the overhead doors. Five type III cutoff luminaires with 150-W high pressure sodium lamps light the entire lot and control glare. The five luminaires are mounted 25-ft high, three on the wall above the canopy and two atop poles at the edge of the lot.

FL/75W T12   HPS/150W

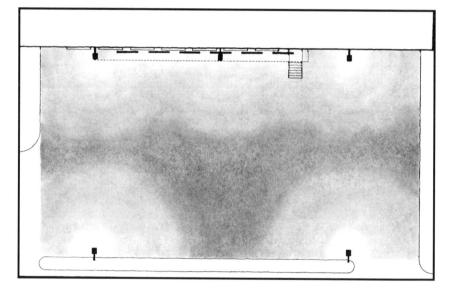

0   25 ft

Sense of Security	Appearance	Initial Equipment Cost	Annual Cost		Average Horizontal Illuminance	Connected Load
			Maintenance	Energy		
★★★★★	★★★★	$4700	$89	$650	2.5 fc	1500 W

LUMBER YARD

B uilding materials are stored both inside the warehouse and around the yard. A fence protects against theft.

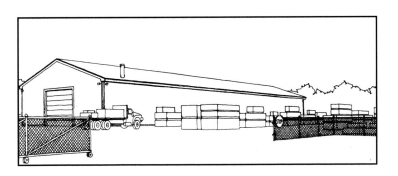

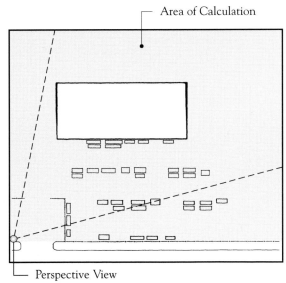

Area of Calculation

Perspective View

	Sense of Security	Appearance	Initial Equipment Cost	Annual Cost	
				Maintenance	Energy
Typical (p. 72)	★	★	—	$460	$1800
Upgrade (p. 73)	★★	★★	$5700	$120	$570
Redesign (p. 74)	★★★★	★★	$9800	$170	$1400

Key: ★ Poorest ★★★★★ Best

Typical

The lumber yard leases a single cobra-head with a 250-W high pressure sodium lamp that the utility installed on a 35-ft pole next to the fence. Eight halogen flood lights with 500-W tubular halogen lamps mounted 19-ft high on the corners of the warehouse, light the rest of yard. Glare from the flood lights makes it difficult for customers and truck drivers to maneuver their vehicles in the yard after dark. Thieves can hide easily in the dark areas near the warehouse entrances and sides and between pallets. The incandescent lamps are expensive to operate and burn out frequently.

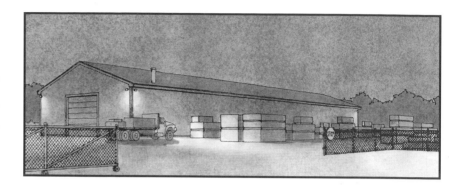

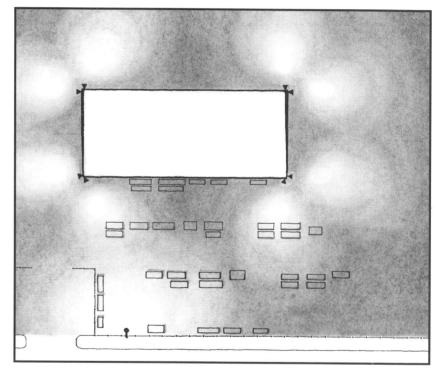

HPS/250W   ▼ TH/500W

0   50 ft

Sense of Security	Appearance	Initial Equipment Cost	Annual Cost		Average Horizontal Illuminance	Connected Load
			Maintenance	Energy		
★	★	—	$460*	$1800	0.49 fc	4000 W

* Lease costs not included.

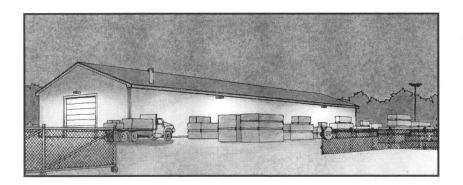

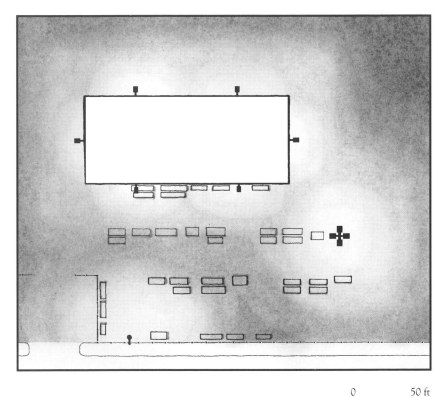

Upgrade

Ten type III cutoffs with 100-W high pressure sodium lamps reduce glare and light pollution. Six are mounted 19-ft high on the warehouse, including one over each of the two building entrances. Four of these luminaires, mounted on a single 35-ft pole, light the yard. The perimeter is still dark, but the warehouse entrances and spaces between the pallets, where most work is done, receive adequate light. The lumber yard continues to lease the cobrahead.

HPS/250W   HPS/100W

0   50 ft

Sense of Security	Appearance	Initial Equipment Cost	Annual Cost		Average Horizontal Illuminance	Connected Load
			Maintenance	Energy		
★★	★★	$5700	$120*	$570	0.53 fc	1300 W

* Lease costs not included.

Redesign

A type III cutoff with a 150-W high pressure sodium lamp mounted atop a 25-ft pole marks the entrance to the yard and replaces the cobrahead, which the lumber yard no longer leases. Eight forward-throw performance wall packs with 150-W high pressure sodium lamps are mounted 19-ft high on the warehouse. Three flood lights with 250-W high pressure sodium lamps mounted on 35-ft poles along the fence, improve the coverage of the yard. The lumber yard took care to aim these luminaires away from the road.

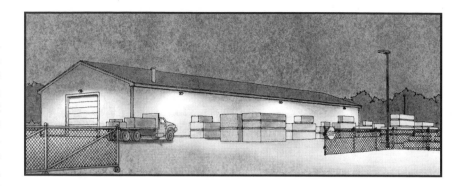

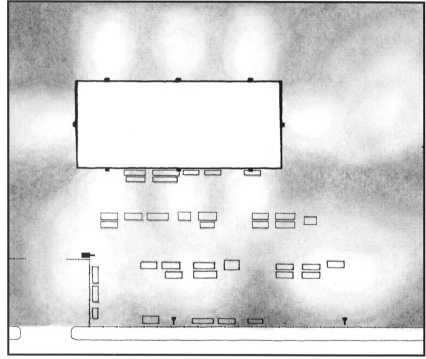

0   50 ft

Sense of Security	Appearance	Initial Equipment Cost	Annual Cost		Average Horizontal Illuminance	Connected Load
			Maintenance	Energy		
★★★★	★★	$9800	$170	$1400	0.99 fc	3200 W

SELF STORAGE

*D*ay and night, renters of self-storage cubicles or garages drive their cars or trucks between rows of these low buildings. Often no one else is around while they load or unload their possessions.

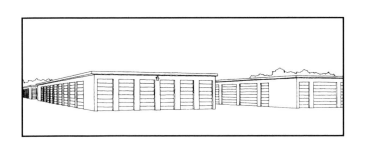

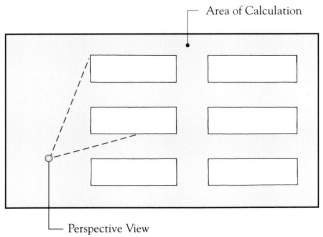

Area of Calculation

Perspective View

	Sense of Security	Appearance	Initial Equipment Cost	Annual Cost	
				Maintenance	Energy
Typical (p. 76)	★	★	—	$64	$960
Upgrade (p. 77)	★★★	★★★	$12,000	$420	$1900
Redesign (p. 78)	★★★	★★★★	$13,000	$220	$1100
Controls Option (p. 78)	—	—	$14,000	$120	$710

Key: ★ Poorest ★★★★★ Best

Typical

Eleven yard lights with 175-W mercury vapor lamps are mounted $9\frac{1}{2}$-ft high on the sides and ends of the buildings. Because of their low mounting heights, the luminaires leave hiding spots between the buildings and in the yard and create glare.

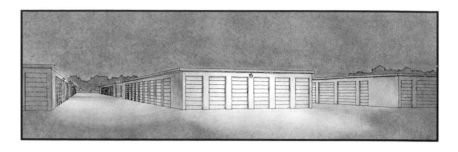

MV/175W

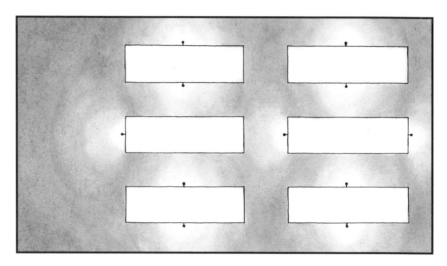

0   75 ft

Sense of Security	Appearance	Initial Equipment Cost	Annual Cost		Average Horizontal Illuminance	Connected Load
			Maintenance	Energy		
★	★	—	$64	$960	0.34 fc	2200 W

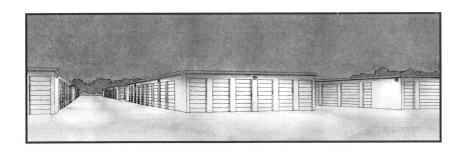

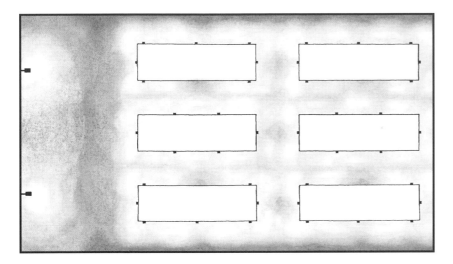

Upgrade

Forty shielded wall packs with 70-W high pressure sodium lamps replace the existing 11 yard lights and are installed in 29 new locations, 9½-ft high on the walls, improving uniformity. Two type III cutoffs with 250-W high pressure sodium lamps atop 35-ft poles light the yard.

HPS/70W   HPS/250W

0   75 ft

Sense of Security	Appearance	Initial Equipment Cost	Annual Cost		Average Horizontal Illuminance	Connected Load
			Maintenance	Energy		
★★★	★★★	$12,000	$420	$1900	0.99 fc	4400 W

Redesign

Forty-four fluorescent sign lighters with 4-ft 40-W T12 RE741 fluorescent lamps are mounted $9^1/_2$-ft high on the building walls. Two type III cutoffs with 250-W high pressure sodium lamps atop 35-ft poles light the yard.

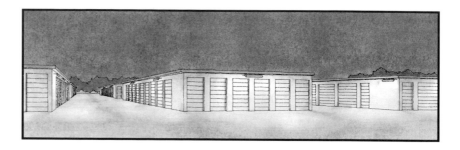

Controls Option

The two type III cutoffs and the 18 perimeter fluorescent sign lighters are on all night to give passersby and potential renters an impression of an open, well-lighted facility. Motion sensors operate the 26 sign lighters between the buildings, reducing their usage to an average of two hours per night. The motion sensors automatically turn on the lights when anyone walks between the buildings.

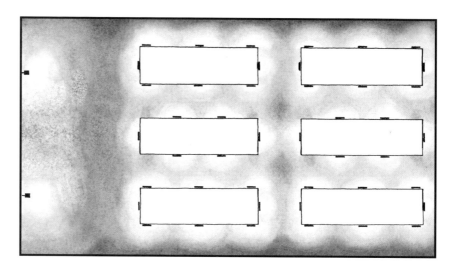

 FL/40W T12   HPS/250W

0 ⊢━━━━━⊣ 75 ft

	Sense of Security	Appearance	Initial uipment Cost	Annual Cost		Average Horizontal Illuminance	Connected Load
				Maintenance	Energy		
Redesign	★★★	★★★★	3,000	$220	$1100	0.98 fc	2600 W
Controls Option	—	—	4,000	$120	$710	0.57 fc*	—

* Illuminance when motion-switched luminaires are off.

GUARDHOUSE

V ehicles approach and stop at the guardhouse. The guard registers the vehicle and gives the driver directions and a visitor's pass.

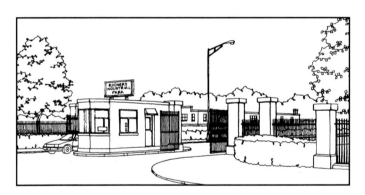

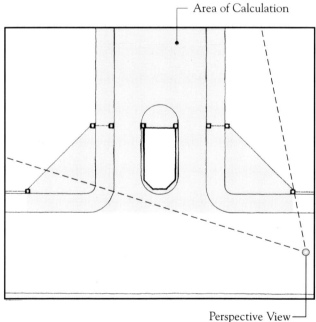

Area of Calculation

Perspective View

	Sense of Security	Appearance	Initial Equipment Cost	Annual Cost	
				Maintenance	Energy
Typical (p. 80)	★	★	—	$0	$0
Upgrade (p. 81)	★★★	★★	$200	$17	$60
Redesign (p. 82)	★★★★	★★★	$4400	$110	$390

Key: ★ Poorest ★★★★★ Best

Typical

Three cobrahead street lights with 250-W high pressure sodium lamps on 35-ft poles light the street and the road into the compound. A task lamp lights the guard's work counter. Unless the light can be dimmed, the bright interior will prevent the guard from seeing outside. The vehicle and the guardhouse create a shadow where the vehicles stop, making it difficult for the guard to see the driver.

HPS/250W

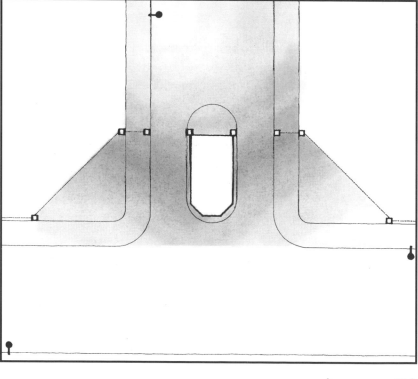

0   25 ft

Sense of Security	Appearance	Initial Equipment Cost	Annual Cost		Average Horizontal Illuminance	Connected Load
			Maintenance	Energy		
★	★	—	$0	$0	1.0 fc	—

Upgrade

An enclosed fluorescent strip with a 4-ft 32-W T8 RE741 fluorescent lamp is mounted on each side of the guardhouse to make it easier to see into the vehicles. The enclosed strips are mounted 10-ft high, above the guardhouse windows, to minimize direct glare for the drivers. Personnel inside the guardhouse have access to a dimmable task light, which can be adjusted to allow guards to see and easily identify vehicles and persons trying to gain entry. The cobrahead street lights remain.

◼ FL/32W T8   ⬤ HPS/250W

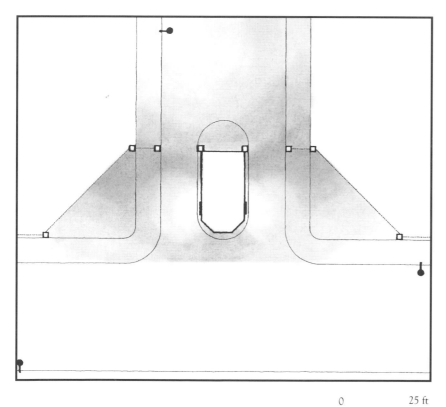

0   25 ft

Sense of Security	Appearance	Initial Equipment Cost	Annual Cost		Average Horizontal Illuminance	Connected Load
			Maintenance	Energy		
★★★	★★	$200	$17	$60	1.4 fc	140 W

Redesign

Four type III cutoffs with 150-W metal halide lamps atop 15-ft poles light the vehicle inspection area. White paint on the pavement where the vehicles stop increases the reflected light. Painting the guardhouse white would further increase the reflected light. An enclosed fluorescent strip with a 4-ft 32-W T8 RE741 fluorescent lamp is mounted on each side of the guardhouse to make it easier to see into the vehicles. Personnel inside the guardhouse have access to a dimmable task light, which can be adjusted to allow guards to see and easily identify vehicles and persons trying to gain entry. The cobrahead street lights remain.

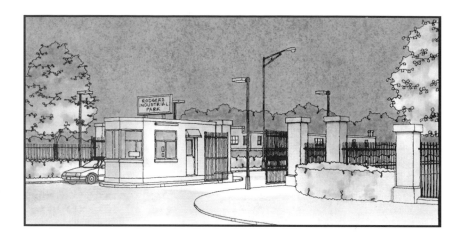

MH/150W   FL/32W T8   HPS/250W

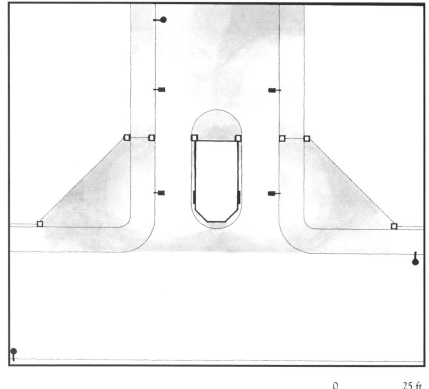

0   25 ft

Sense of Security	Appearance	Initial Equipment Cost	Annual Cost		Average Horizontal Illuminance	Connected Load
			Maintenance	Energy		
★★★★	★★★	$4400	$110*	$390	4.3 fc	900 W

* Does not includes painting.

GATEHOUSE

*S*igns mark the entrances to parks, campuses, and residential communities. People stop at the kiosk for directions or to show their passes.

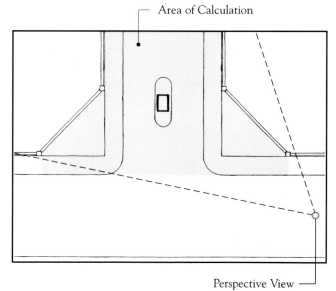

Area of Calculation

Perspective View

	Sense of Security	Appearance	Initial Equipment Cost	Annual Cost	
				Maintenance	Energy
Typical (p. 84)	★	★	—	$150	$260
Upgrade (p. 85)	★★★	★★★	$1100	$99	$140
Redesign (p. 86)	★★★★★	★★★★	$2500	$120	$290

Key: ★ Poorest   ★★★★★ Best

Typical

A two-headed PAR lamp holder mounted on the ground directs light from two 150-W PAR lamps toward each of the signs; however, drivers and pedestrians are bothered by the stray light. Only the nearby cobrahead street lights with 250-W high pressure sodium lamps on 35-ft poles light the street. Not much light reaches the kiosk. The attendant's desk has a dimmable task light.

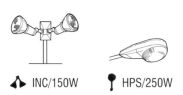

INC/150W   HPS/250W

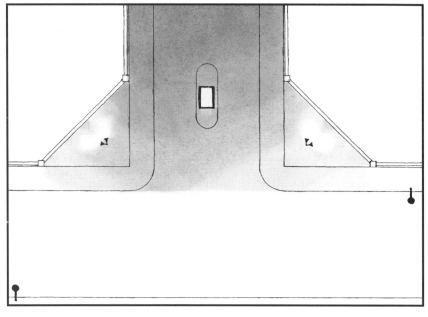

0   25 ft

Sense of Security	Appearance	Initial Equipment Cost	Annual Cost		Average Horizontal Illuminance	Connected Load
			Maintenance	Energy		
★	★	—	$150	$260	0.46 fc	600 W

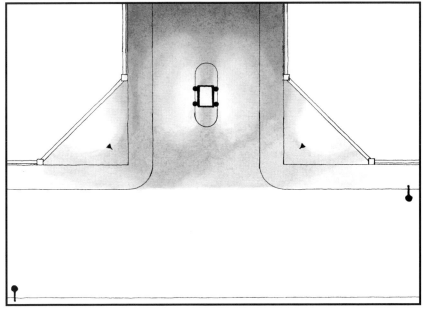

0   25 ft

Upgrade

A ground-mounted flood light with a 70-W metal halide lamp lights each of the signs. These luminaires direct the light horizontally across the signs. Optional shielding hoods reduce glare. Visitors identify the kiosk because four wall-mounted decorative surface luminaires with 28-W dedicated compact fluorescent lamps are mounted 6-ft high on its surface to help the structure stand out. To minimize glare, the decorative surface luminaires are positioned as far away from the information window as possible. The cobrahead street lights and dimmable task light remain.

▼ HPS/70W   • CFL/28W   ⚲ HPS/250W

Sense of Security	Appearance	Initial Equipment Cost	Annual Cost		Average Horizontal Illuminance	Connected Load
			Maintenance	Energy		
★★★	★★★	$1100	$99	$140	1.0 fc	320 W

Redesign

Four fluorescent sign lighters highlight each of the entrance signs. Each luminaire houses a 4-ft 32-W T8 RE741 fluorescent lamp and is mounted 6-ft high. Two performance post tops with 100-W metal halide lamps on 12-ft poles complement the light from the four decorative surface luminaires with 28-W dedicated compact fluorescent lamps, which are mounted 6-ft high on the kiosk. The cobrahead street lights and dimmable task light remain.

 FL/32W T8   CFL/28W   MH/100W

 HPS/250W

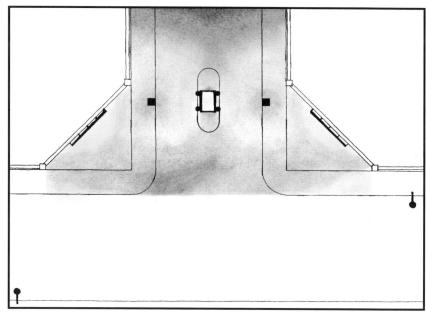

0   25 ft

Sense of Security	Appearance	Initial Equipment Cost	Annual Cost		Average Horizontal Illuminance	Connected Load
			Maintenance	Energy		
★★★★★	★★★★	$2500	$120	$290	2.3 fc	650 W

POCKET PARK

*P*eople rest from shopping and eat lunch on the benches of this pocket park during the day, but avoid the park at night, fearing the crime and vandals.

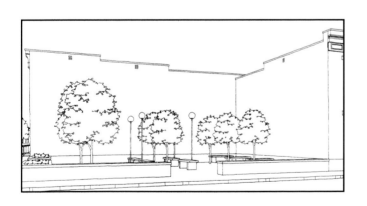

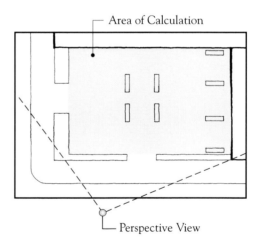

Area of Calculation

Perspective View

	Sense of Security	Appearance	Initial Equipment Cost	Annual Cost	
				Maintenance	Energy
Typical (p. 88)	★	★	—	$34	$220
Upgrade 1 (p. 89)	★★	★★★	$1800	$100	$90
Upgrade 2 (p. 90)	★★★	★★★	$2000	$170	$250
Redesign (p. 91)	★★★★★	★★★★	$5700	$190	$440

Key: ★ Poorest ★★★★★ Best

Typical

Four old decorative post tops with 100-W mercury lamps on 10-ft poles at the center of the park have all yellowed and now produce much less light than they did when new. A nearby cobra-head street light with a 250-W high pressure sodium lamp on a 35-ft pole contributes some light to the park.

● MV/100W ⬤ HPS/250W

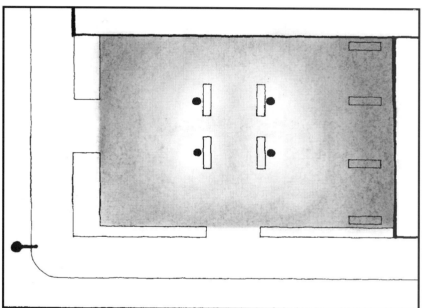

0   10 ft

Sense of Security	Appearance	Initial Equipment Cost	Annual Cost		Average Horizontal Illuminance	Connected Load
			Maintenance	Energy		
★	★	—	$34	$220	0.57 fc	500 W

Upgrade 1

Six performance post tops with 32-W compact fluorescent lamps and low-temperature electronic ballasts improve uniformity and double light levels. Four of these luminaires are mounted on the existing 10-ft poles and two are wall mounted 10-ft high. The cobrahead street light remains.

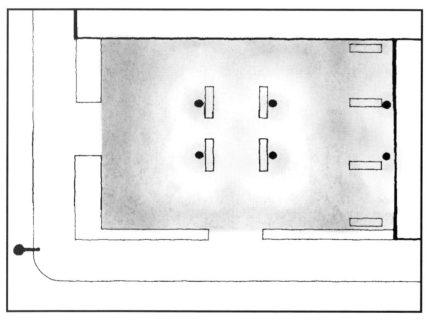

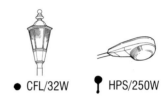

● CFL/32W   ● HPS/250W

0   10 ft

Sense of Security	Appearance	Initial Equipment Cost	Annual Cost		Average Horizontal Illuminance	Connected Load
			Maintenance	Energy		
★★	★★★	$1800	$100	$90	1.1 fc	200 W

Upgrade 2

The city classifies the park as a security risk area and approves the park owner's application for a waiver of the the lighting power limits of the energy code. This action permits the installation of six performance post top luminaires with 70-W metal halide lamps mounted 10-ft high, improving the illuminance level. The cobrahead street light remains.

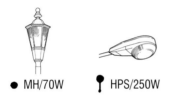

● MH/70W   ⦿ HPS/250W

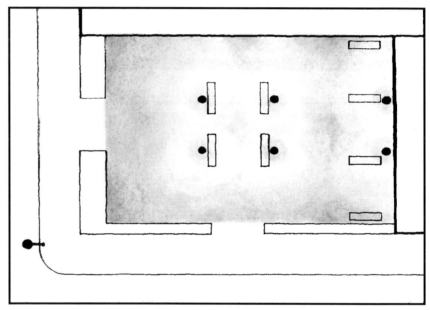

0   10 ft

Sense of Security	Appearance	Initial Equipment Cost	Annual Cost		Average Horizontal Illuminance	Connected Load
			Maintenance	Energy		
★★★	★★★	$2000	$170	$250	2.1 fc	570 W

Redesign

The city classifies the park as a security risk area and approves the park owner's application for a waiver of the the lighting power limits of the energy code. Four decorative cutoffs with 100-W metal halide lamps flank the entrances atop 10-ft poles. Four downlight wall luminaires, also with 100-W metal halide lamps and mounted 15-ft high on the building, complete the excellent site coverage. The cobrahead street light remains.

● MH/100W   ▬ MH/100W   ♀ HPS/250W

0   10 ft

Sense of Security	Appearance	Initial Equipment Cost	Annual Cost		Average Horizontal Illuminance	Connected Load
			Maintenance	Energy		
★★★★★	★★★★	$5700	$190	$440	7.4 fc	1000 W

PLAYGROUND

C hildren of all ages play on the swings, basketball courts, and other facilities of this town park. Parents and babysitters return home with younger children before the sun sets while older children sometimes play unsupervised until dusk or later.

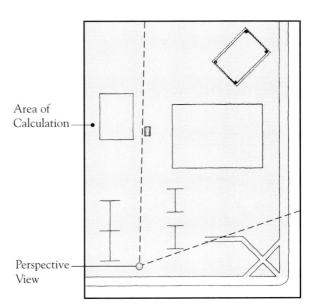

Area of Calculation

Perspective View

	Sense of Security	Appearance	Initial Equipment Cost	Annual Cost	
				Maintenance	Energy
Typical (p. 94)	★	★	—	$82	$220
Upgrade (p. 95)	★★	★★	$980	$29	$200
Redesign 1 (p. 96)	★★★★	★★★★	$7000	$250	$1100
Redesign 2 (p. 97)	★★	★★★	$4500	$60	$570
Controls Option (p. 97)	—	—	$4500	$29	$270

Key: ★ Poorest ★★★★★ Best

Typical

A yard light with a 175-W mercury lamp atop a 20-ft pole provides only a little light on the basketball court and leaves many hiding areas. A two-headed PAR lamp holder mounted 10-ft high on the pavilion's trusses holds two 150-W PAR lamps.

  MV/175W   INC/150W

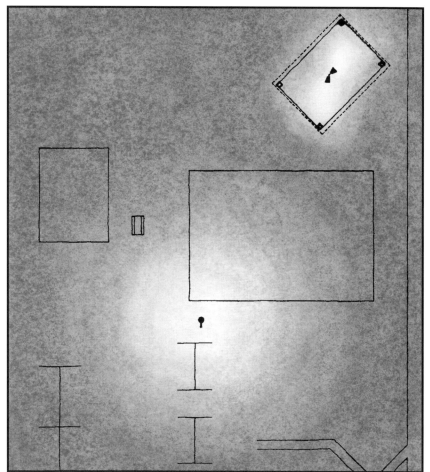

 0   40 ft

Sense of Security	Appearance	Initial Equipment Cost	Annual Cost		Average Horizontal Illuminance	Connected Load
			Maintenance	Energy		
★	★	—	$82	$220	0.11 fc	500 W

Upgrade

Two type III cutoffs with 150-W high pressure sodium lamps replace the yard light on the existing 20-ft pole, reducing the glare and extending the area that is effectively lighted. The PAR lamp holder is replaced with an enclosed fluorescent strip with an 8-ft 75-W slimline T12 RE741 fluorescent lamp.

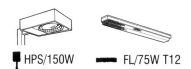

HPS/150W   FL/75W T12

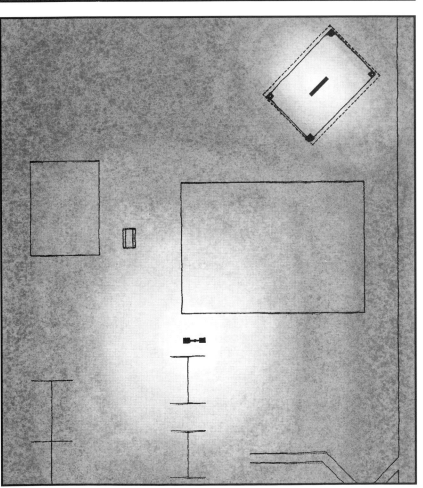

0   40 ft

Sense of Security	Appearance	Initial Equipment Cost	Annual Cost		Average Horizontal Illuminance	Connected Load
			Maintenance	Energy		
★★	★★	$980	$29	$200	0.41 fc	470 W

Redesign 1

Seven type III cutoffs with 250-W metal halide lamps are mounted on five 20-ft poles at the sides of the basketball court and the edges of the park. Two performance post tops with 100-W metal halide lamps on 10-ft poles light the corner entrance. An enclosed fluorescent strip with an 8-ft 75-W slimline T12 RE741 fluorescent lamp lights the pavilion.

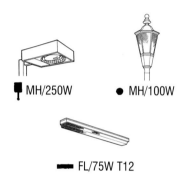

MH/250W   ● MH/100W

━ FL/75W T12

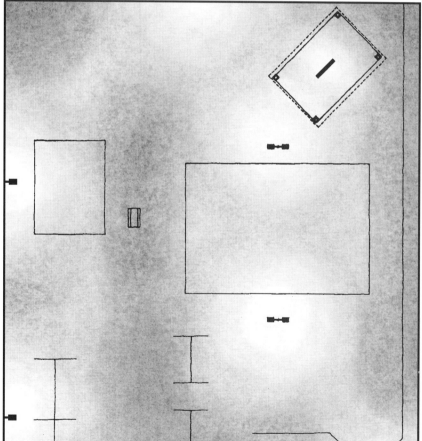

0   40 ft

Sense of Security	Appearance	Initial Equipment Cost	Annual Cost		Average Horizontal Illuminance	Connected Load
			Maintenance	Energy		
★★★★	★★★★	$7000	$250	$1100	1.2 fc	2400 W

Redesign 2

Wanting to provide supervised outdoor activity after dark for the neighborhood's teens and young adults, the parks committee concentrated on lighting the basketball court. Four 20-ft poles positioned along two of the court's edges each provide a mounting position for a type III cutoff with a 250-W high pressure sodium lamp. An enclosed fluorescent strip with an 8-ft 75-W slimline T12 RE741 fluorescent lamp lights the pavilion.

Controls Option

A time clock switches off three of the type III cutoff luminaires at midnight. These three luminaires remain off all winter, when it is too cold to play basketball at night. Town maintenance personnel monitor the fourth luminaire to ensure timely lamp replacement because that luminaire is left on many hours more than the other three.

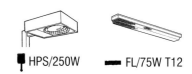

HPS/250W   FL/75W T12

0   40 ft

	Sense of Security	Appearance	Initial Equipment Cost	Annual Cost		Average Horizontal Illuminance	Connected Load
				Maintenance	Energy		
Redesign 2	★★	★★★	$4500	$60	$570	1.2 fc	1300 W
Controls Option	—	—	$4500	$29	$270	0.30 fc*	—

* Illuminance when time-clock-switched luminaires are off.

CAMPUS GREEN

*S*everal college buildings overlook a park-like open green. Even at night, students and visitors walk along the paths.

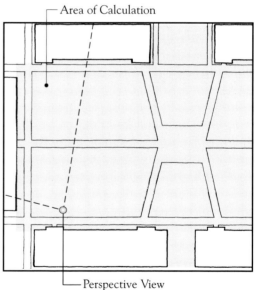

Area of Calculation

Perspective View

	Sense of Security	Appearance	Initial Equipment Cost	Annual Cost	
				Maintenance	Energy
Typical (p. 100)	★★	★★	—	$97	$1100
Upgrade (p. 101)	★★★	★★★★	$19,000	$840	$2000
Redesign (p. 102)	★★★★	★★★★★	$43,000	$900	$3200

Key: ★ Poorest ★★★★★ Best

Typical

The 16-ft poles at the nine intersections of the paths each support a decorative post top with a 175-W mercury vapor lamp. The decorative post tops lose light to the sky and create glare that makes it hard to see into the dark areas between the luminaires, especially against a background of dark buildings. Four wall packs with 150-W high pressure sodium lamps are interspersed throughout the green, mounted 15-ft high on building walls.

 MV/175W   HPS/150W

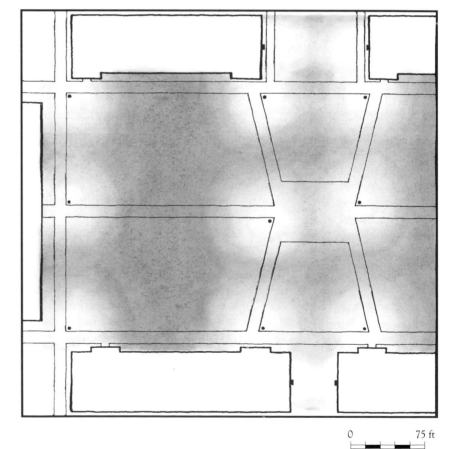

0   75 ft

Sense of Security	Appearance	Initial Equipment Cost	Annual Cost		Average Horizontal Illuminance	Connected Load
			Maintenance	Energy		
★★	★★	—	$97	$1100	0.33 fc	2600 W

Upgrade

Seventeen new 16-ft poles and the nine existing poles provide locations for 26 performance post tops with 100-W metal halide lamps. The performance post tops light the paths uniformly and with less light pollution. Four shielded wall packs with 100-W metal halide lamps replace the existing wall packs, reducing glare. The good color rendition of the metal halide lamps improves the appearance of the campus at night.

● MH/100W   ▰ MH/100W

0   75 ft

Sense of Security	Appearance	Initial Equipment Cost	Annual Cost		Average Horizontal Illuminance	Connected Load
			Maintenance	Energy		
★★★	★★★★	$19,000	$840	$2000	0.61 fc	4600 W

Redesign

Twenty-nine decorative cutoffs with 150-W metal halide lamps atop 20-ft poles line the paths and light between the buildings. The luminaires emphasize the central gathering space. Four grade-mounted flood lights with 250-W metal halide lamps illuminate the wings of the main building. Four additional flood lights with 100-W metal halide lamps illuminate the center section of the building from the bases of the columns above the entrance. These luminaires light the facade of this building, adding focus and a sense of brightness to the campus. Two wall-mounted decorative surface luminaires with 28-W compact fluorescent lamps identify the doorways.

• MH/150W   ◄ MH/250W   ◆ CFL/28W

 MH/100W

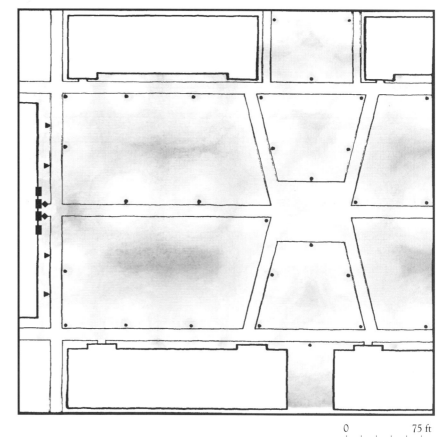

0   75 ft

Sense of Security	Appearance	Initial Equipment Cost	Annual Cost		Average Horizontal Illuminance	Connected Load
			Maintenance	Energy		
★★★★	★★★★★	$43,000	$900	$3200	1.5 fc	7300 W

MUNICIPAL PARK

B y day, people enjoy the lawns, foliage, ponds, and the convenience of rest rooms in this municipal park. People stroll through the park at night for enjoyment or use it as a shortcut to local destinations.

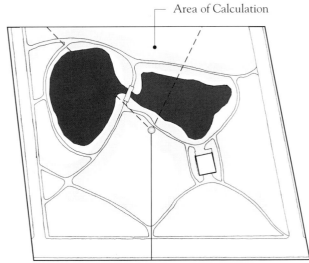

Perspective View

	Sense of Security	Appearance	Initial Equipment Cost	Annual Cost	
				Maintenance	Energy
Typical (p. 104)	★	★	—	$100	$140
Upgrade (p. 105)	★★★	★★★	$15,000	$350	$1100
Redesign (p. 106)	★★★★	★★★★★	$42,000	$800	$2800

Key: ★ Poorest ★★★★★ Best

Typical

From atop a 20-ft pole, a yard light with a 175-W mercury vapor lamp lights a small area near the bridge. A decorative surface luminaire with a 60-W A-lamp is mounted 8-ft high on each gable, just above the rest rooms. The authorities are concerned about the darkness of most of the paths. Eight cobrahead street lights with 250-W high pressure sodium lamps on 35-ft poles light the adjoining streets.

♦ HPS/250W   ◆ MV/175W   • INC/60W

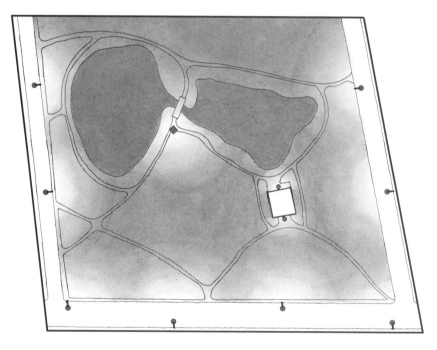

0   125 ft

Sense of Security	Appearance	Initial Equipment Cost	Annual Cost		Average Horizontal Illuminance	Connected Load
			Maintenance	Energy		
★	★	—	$100	$140	0.06 fc*	320 W

* Illuminance on major paths.

Upgrade

Thirteen type III cutoffs with 150-W metal halide lamps light the major paths. The luminaires are mounted atop the existing pole and 12 new 20-ft poles. The two cutoff luminaires near the rest rooms could have been mounted on the building, were it taller. Four decorative surface luminaires with 20-W dedicated compact fluorescent lamps wall mounted 8-ft high replace the incandescent surface luminaires on the building. The eight cobrahead street lights remain.

HPS/250W   MH/150W   • CFL/20W

0   125 ft

Sense of Security	Appearance	Initial Equipment Cost	Annual Cost		Average Horizontal Illuminance	Connected Load
			Maintenance	Energy		
★★★	★★★	$15,000	$350	$1100	0.74 fc*	2600 W

* Illuminance on major paths.

Redesign

Thirty-three period-style decorative cutoffs with 150-W metal halide lamps are mounted atop 15-ft poles that line the paths. The period luminaires and 15-ft poles provide good uniformity and illuminance along the path. The luminaires are wonderfully scaled to the size and uses of the park. A decorative surface luminaire with a 20-W compact fluorescent lamp is mounted 8-ft high on each gable end of the building. The eight cobrahead street lights remain.

 HPS/250W   MH/150W   CFL/20W

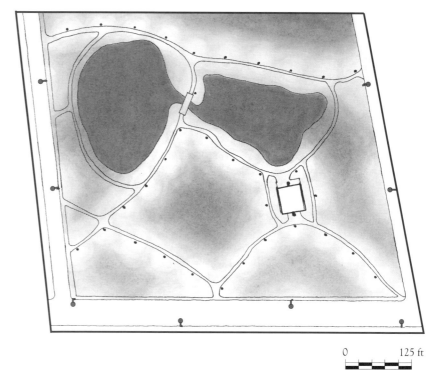

0   125 ft

Sense of Security	Appearance	Initial Equipment Cost	Annual Cost		Average Horizontal Illuminance	Connected Load
			Maintenance	Energy		
★★★★	★★★★★	$42,000	$800	$2800	1.4 fc*	6300 W

* Illuminance on major paths.

WATERFRONT WALK

Waterfront walks often line the shores of rivers, lakes, and oceans. People walk the paths at the water's edge and stop at benches, separated from the city by lawns, trees, or plantings.

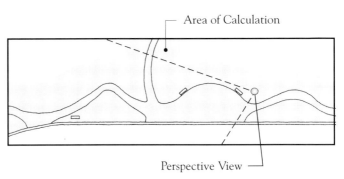

Area of Calculation

Perspective View

	Sense of Security	Appearance	Initial Equipment Cost	Annual Cost	
				Maintenance	Energy
Typical (p. 108)	★	★	—	$34	$220
Upgrade (p. 109)	★★	★★★	$3200	$160	$380
Redesign (p. 110)	★★★★	★★★★	$9400	$260	$370

Key: ★ Poorest ★★★★★ Best

Typical

Four decorative post tops with 100-W mercury vapor lamps mounted on 10-ft poles produce little light and leave large dark spots. The yellowed old spheres lose light to the sky and create glare that detracts from the natural views. The park entrance is dark.

● MV/100W

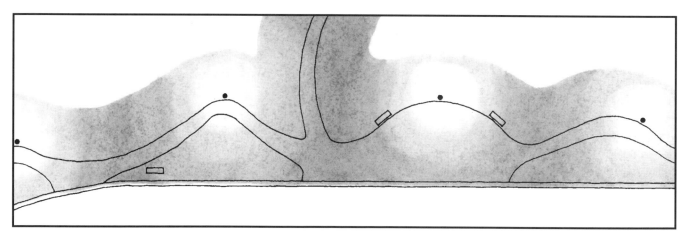

0   30 ft

Sense of Security	Appearance	Initial Equipment Cost	Annual Cost		Average Horizontal Illuminance	Connected Load
			Maintenance	Energy		
★	★	—	$34	$220	0.06 fc*	500 W

* Illuminance on major paths.

Upgrade

Seven performance post tops with 100-W metal halide lamps improve the color of the grass, shrubs, and trees as well as the coverage along the paths. Four of these post tops are mounted on the existing poles and three are atop new 10-ft poles. The additional poles decrease the spacing between luminaires, reducing the size of dark areas. The entrance to the park remains dark.

● MH/100W

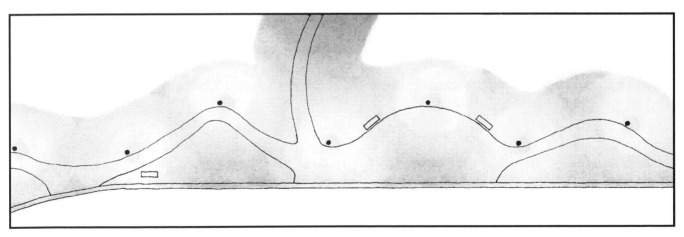

0   30 ft

Sense of Security	Appearance	Initial Equipment Cost	Annual Cost		Average Horizontal Illuminance	Connected Load
			Maintenance	Energy		
★★	★★★	$3200	$160	$380	0.47 fc*	880 W

* Illuminance on major paths.

Redesign

Nine performance post tops with 70-W metal halide lamps atop 12-ft poles improve the path lighting and mark the park entrance. Eight 3-ft high bollards with 32-W compact fluorescent lamps and low-temperature electronic ballasts delineate the water's edge for safety, while creating a decorative effect.

MH/70W   • CFL/32W

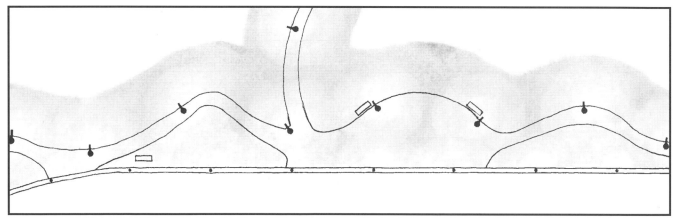

0   30 ft

Sense of Security	Appearance	Initial Equipment Cost	Annual Cost		Average Horizontal Illuminance	Connected Load
			Maintenance	Energy		
★★★★	★★★★	$9400	$260	$370	0.70 fc*	1100 W

* Illuminance on major paths.

SCHOOL 1

*P*arents and school buses drop off and pick up children at the main entrance of this three-story school. Neighborhood groups, parents, and the school's teams and clubs sometimes return after dark for meetings and events. The original building may be as much as 70 years old. The addition is much more recent. School officials worry about vandalism and crime on the school's grounds.

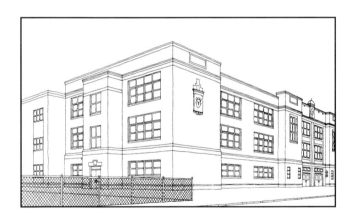

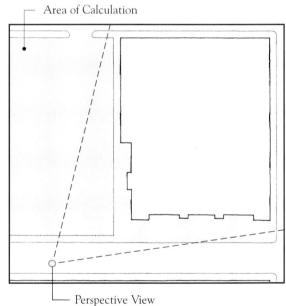

Area of Calculation

Perspective View

	Sense of Security	Appearance	Initial Equipment Cost	Annual Cost	
				Maintenance	Energy
Typical (p. 112)	★	★	—	$150	$250
Upgrade (p. 113)	★★	★★★	$3000	$110	$440
Redesign 1 (p. 114)	★★★★	★★★	$7700	$200	$1400
Redesign 2 (p. 115)	★★★★	★★★★	$10,000	$400	$1800

Key: ★ Poorest   ★★★★★ Best

Typical

Two decorative surface luminaires with 100-W A-lamps mark the school's street entrance. These old and dirty period lanterns, mounted 8-ft high, do little to light the school's perimeter. Only two wall packs with 150-W high pressure sodium lamps mounted 13-ft high on the wall light the schoolyard. Three cobrahead street lights with 250-W high pressure sodium lamps on 35-ft poles light the street.

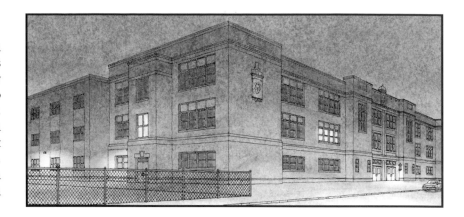

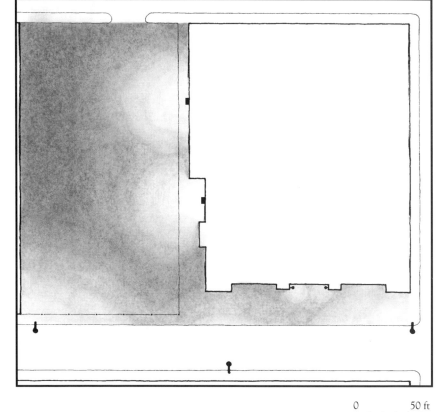

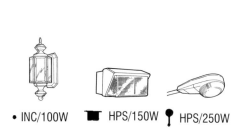

• INC/100W　◼ HPS/150W　♀ HPS/250W

0　　　50 ft

Sense of Security	Appearance	Initial Equipment Cost	Annual Cost		Average Horizontal Illuminance	Connected Load
			Maintenance	Energy		
★	★	—	$150	$250	0.41 fc	580 W

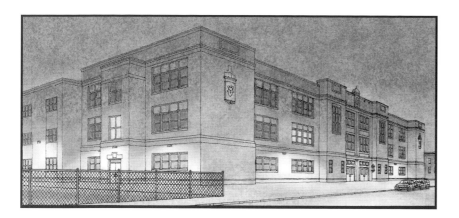

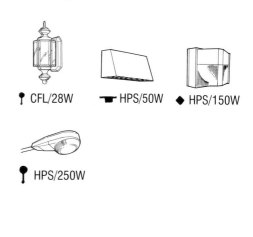

Upgrade

Frosted, impact-resistant acrylic replaces the clear glass in the panels of the two wall-mounted, period decorative surface luminaires, which are cleaned and rewired for 28-W dedicated compact fluorescent lamps. Six downlight wall luminaires with 50-W high pressure sodium lamps mounted 13-ft high on the original building light the perimeter. One of the downlight wall luminaires reuses a mounting position. Three forward-throw performance wall packs with 150-W high pressure sodium lamps replace the wall pack on the addition. These luminaires light more of the site, but are far enough from adjoining properties to avoid glare and light trespass. Mounted 20-ft high and with a forward-throw distribution, these luminaires improve the lighting uniformity in the schoolyard. The cobrahead street lights remain.

	CFL/28W		HPS/50W		HPS/150W

HPS/250W

0   50 ft

Sense of Security	Appearance	Initial Equipment Cost	Annual Cost		Average Horizontal Illuminance	Connected Load
			Maintenance	Energy		
★★	★★★	$3000	$110	$440	0.68 fc	1000 W

Redesign 1

Decorative wall-mounted period lanterns with 28-W compact fluorescent lamps mark the street entrance. Eleven front-shielded wall packs, which distribute light upwards and downwards, with 50-W high pressure sodium lamps, are mounted 13-ft high on the original building to light the perimeter. Five forward-throw type III cutoffs with 400-W high pressure sodium lamps light the schoolyard. Three of the type III cutoffs are mounted 35-ft high on the addition and two on 35-ft poles near the side fence. If the owner had agreed, the pole-mounted luminaires could have been mounted on the adjacent building. The cobra-head street lights remain.

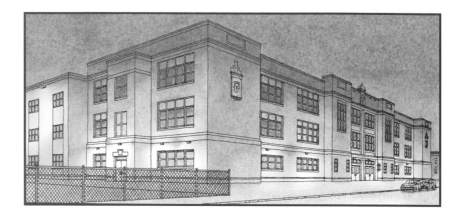

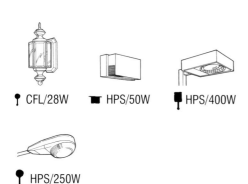

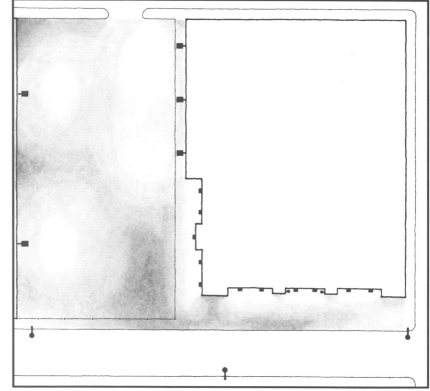

0   50 ft

Sense of Security	Appearance	Initial Equipment Cost	Annual Cost		Average Horizontal Illuminance	Connected Load
			Maintenance	Energy		
★★★★	★★★	$7700	$200	$1400	2.7 fc	3100 W

Redesign 2

Two decorative wall-mounted period lanterns with 28-W compact fluorescent lamps mark the main entrance. Ten front-shielded wall packs with 70-W metal halide lamps mounted 13-ft high on the original building light the perimeter. Four wall-mounted and three pole-mounted forward-throw type III cutoffs with 400-W metal halide lamps improve the color and uniformity in the yard from the 35-ft high positions. The cobrahead street lights remain.

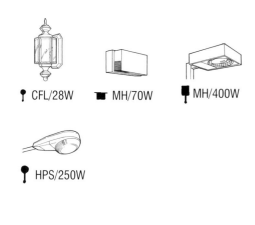

CFL/28W   MH/70W   MH/400W

HPS/250W

0   50 ft

Sense of Security	Appearance	Initial Equipment Cost	Annual Cost		Average Horizontal Illuminance	Connected Load
			Maintenance	Energy		
★★★★	★★★★	$10,000	$400	$1800	2.3 fc	4200 W

SCHOOL 2

*O*pen areas, such as fields or parking lots surround this one-story school. Children may wait at the main entrance for their rides home after an athletic event or meeting.

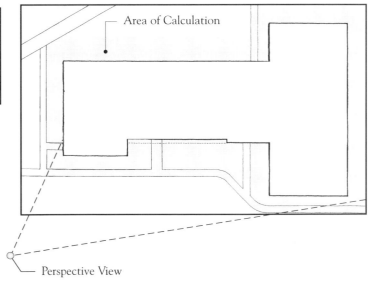

Area of Calculation

Perspective View

	Sense of Security	Appearance	Initial Equipment Cost	Annual Cost	
				Maintenance	Energy
Typical (p. 118)	★	★	—	$1000	$1000
Upgrade 1 (p. 119)	★★★	★★	$4100	$270	$1100
Upgrade 2 (p. 119)	★★★	★★★	$4300	$470	$1000
Redesign (p. 120)	★★★★	★★★	$8000	$420	$1400

Key: ★ Poorest ★★★★★ Best

Typical

Seven wall packs with 150-W high pressure sodium lamps provide some lighting around the school's perimeter but leave dark spots and create glare. Two of these wall packs are mounted 25-ft high on the gymnasium. The others are mounted 12-ft high, which limits the area they light. The 100-W A-lamps in the ten incandescent downlights under the 8-ft high overhang frequently burn out.

HPS/150W   • INC/100W

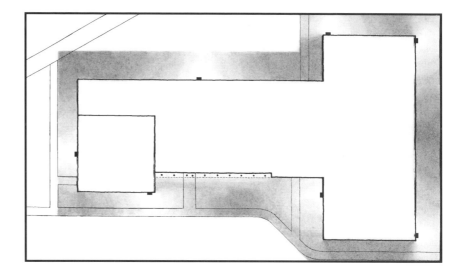

0   75 ft

Sense of Security	Appearance	Initial Equipment Cost	Annual Cost		Average Horizontal Illuminance	Connected Load
			Maintenance	Energy		
★	★	—	$1000	$1000	0.77 fc	2300 W

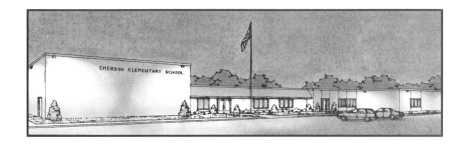

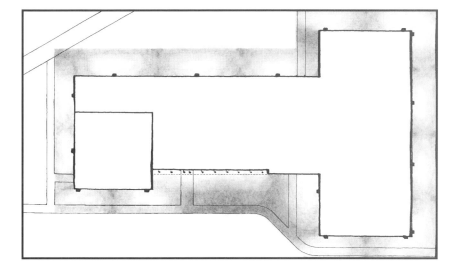

0   75 ft

Upgrade 1

Sixteen side-throw performance wall packs with 100-W HPS lamps light the perimeter of the building. Thirteen of these luminaires are mounted 12-ft high on the main building, and three are mounted 25-ft high on the gymnasium. The existing locations provide suitable mounting positions for seven of the luminaires: eight new 12-ft high mounting positions and one new 25-ft high position accommodate the additional new luminaires. Ten performance versions of the decorative surface luminaire with 28-W compact fluorescent lamps replace the incandescent downlights in the ceiling of the entrance canopy.

Upgrade 2

The use of 100-W metal halide lamps to replace the 100-W HPS lamps in the side-throw performance wall packs improves the color appearance of the school, people's apparel and vehicles, and other objects around the school.

Upgrade 1   🡆 HPS/100W   • CFL/28W
Upgrade 2   MH/100W

	Sense of Security	Appearance	Initial Equipment Cost	Annual Cost		Average Horizontal Illuminance	Connected Load
				Maintenance	Energy		
Upgrade 1	★★★	★★	$4100	$270	$1100	0.99 fc	2400 W
Upgrade 2	★★★	★★★	$4300	$470	$1000	0.88 fc	2300 W

Typical

The city or utility company provides street lights: 250-W high pressure sodium lamps installed in two cobraheads on 35-ft poles. Each home features a decorative surface luminaire with a 60-W A-lamp near its entry. The residents turn these on and off according to their individual schedules and habits; often as many as 13 of the 23 lamps are on at a time. Cars and trees create shadows, especially in the center of the block where the cobraheads provide little light. Basement-level entry stairs can be ominously dark.

HPS/250W   • INC/60W

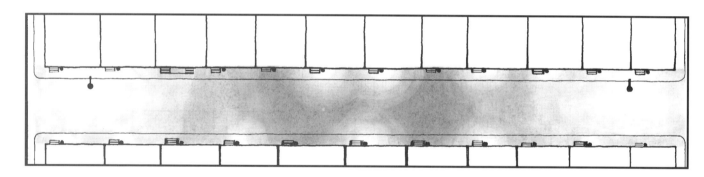

0   50 ft

Sense of Security	Appearance	Initial Equipment Cost	Annual Cost		Average Horizontal Illuminance	Connected Load
			Maintenance	Energy		
★	★★	—	$17*	$100	0.84 fc	1400 W

* Maintenance costs do not include labor.

Upgrade

The neighborhood or civic association installs two decorative surface luminaires with 28-W dedicated compact fluorescent lamps per building, a total of 46. One luminaire replaces the existing entrance light, the other may be over the entrance to a basement. The neighbors have agreed that the luminaires will be switched on and off by integral photocells and will remain on all night. The cobrahead street lights remain unchanged.

HPS/250W   • CFL/28W

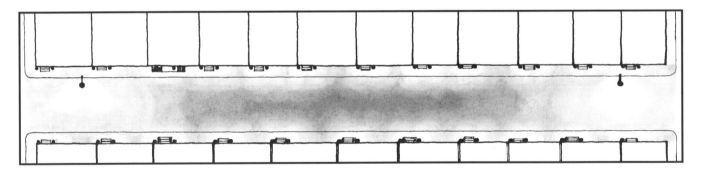

0   50 ft

Sense of Security	Appearance	Initial Equipment Cost	Annual Cost		Average Horizontal Illuminance	Connected Load
			Maintenance	Energy		
★★	★★★	$4100	$280*	$650	1.3 fc	1500 W

* Maintenance costs do not include labor.

Redesign

The neighborhood or civic association adds seven performance post tops with 150-W metal halide lamps. These luminaires, which are mounted on 12-ft poles, light the sidewalk and street without causing glare when viewed from the windows. Twenty-three decorative surface luminaires with integral photocells and dedicated 28-W compact fluorescent lamps are installed near the entrances. Basement stairs that are far from the post tops may need an additional decorative surface luminaire. The cobrahead street lights remain unchanged.

 HPS/250W   • CFL/28W   ■ MH/150W

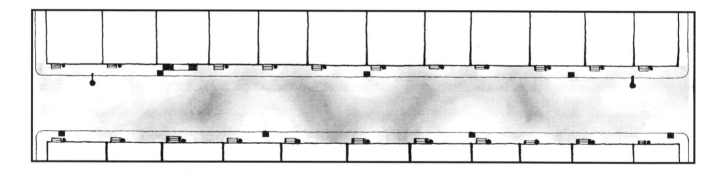

0   50 ft

Sense of Security	Appearance	Initial Equipment Cost	Annual Cost		Average Horizontal Illuminance	Connected Load
			Maintenance	Energy		
★★★★	★★★★	$7100	$290	$900	2.1 fc	2100 W

SMALL APARTMENTS

*T*hree-family apartment buildings line the residential streets of many cities. Tenants park their cars in a narrow common drive and enter the building through doors on the front porch or at the rear of the building.

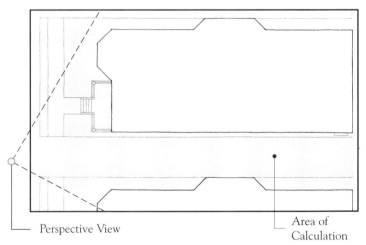

Perspective View   Area of Calculation

	Sense of Security	Appearance	Initial Equipment Cost	Annual Cost	
				Maintenance	Energy
Typical (p. 126)	★	★★	—	$3	$26
Upgrade (p. 127)	★★★	★★	$280	$10	$11
Redesign (p. 128)	★★★★	★★★	$1000	$22	$51

Key: ★ Poorest   ★★★★★ Best

Typical

A decorative surface luminaire with a 100-W A-lamp is mounted on each of the three porch ceilings. A wall-mounted decorative surface luminaire with a 60-W A-lamp is next to the back door. A tenant switches the luminaires from inside the door, leaving them on only two hours per night or so. The driveway is very dark, even when the lights are on. Cobraheads with 250-W high pressure sodium lamps on 35-ft poles light the street.

• INC/100W   INC/60W

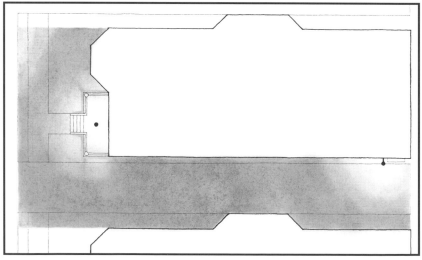

0 ___ 15 ft

Sense of Security	Appearance	Initial Equipment Cost	Annual Cost		Average Horizontal Illuminance	Connected Load
			Maintenance	Energy		
★	★★	—	$3	$26	0.25 fc	360 W

Upgrade

Four 23-W screwbase compact fluorescent lamps replace the incandescent lamps in the decorative surface luminaires on the porch ceilings and next to the back door. Two new decorative surface luminaires with 23-W compact fluorescent lamps are mounted 12-ft high on the side walls. During the two hours nightly when these lamps are on, it is much easier to see people and obstacles in the driveway.

• CFL/23W   CFL/23W

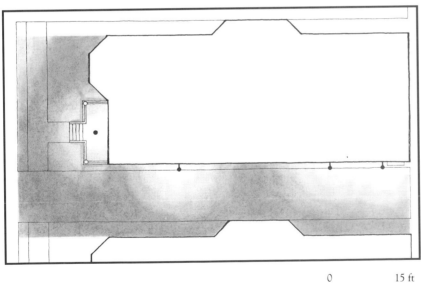

0   15 ft

Sense of Security	Appearance	Initial Equipment Cost	Annual Cost		Average Horizontal Illuminance	Connected Load
			Maintenance	Energy		
★★★	★★	$280	$10	$11	0.49 fc	160 W

Redesign

The three existing positions on the porch ceilings and the one next to the back door are suitable for decorative surface luminaires with 28-W and 20-W dedicated compact fluorescent lamps, respectively. These four luminaires average only two hours of operation each night. Three downlight wall luminaires are switched by photosensors and operate all night. The downlight wall luminaires are mounted 10-ft high on the side wall and contain 28-W dedicated compact fluorescent lamps. These luminaires direct the light to the driveway, not to the windows on the adjacent building.

 • CFL/28W   CFL/20W   CFL/28W

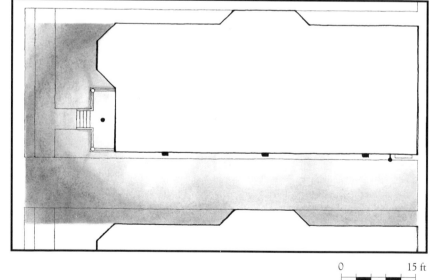

0   15 ft

Sense of Security	Appearance	Initial Equipment Cost	Annual Cost		Average Horizontal Illuminance	Connected Load
			Maintenance	Energy		
★★★★	★★★	$1000	$22	$51	1.2 fc	220 W

GROUP HOUSING

V isitors to this low-rise senior citizen home and its residents approach the main entrance from the parking lot or the sidewalk that connects the building to the city streets.

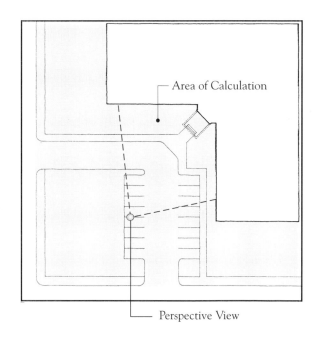

Area of Calculation

Perspective View

	Sense of Security	Appearance	Initial Equipment Cost	Annual Cost	
				Maintenance	Energy
Typical (p. 130)	★	★★	—	$930	$470
Upgrade 1 (p. 131)	★★★	★★	$10,000	$230	$630
Upgrade 2 (p. 131)	★★★	★★★	$10,000	$340	$520
Redesign (p. 132)	★★★★	★★★★	$14,000	$330	$790

Key: ★ Poorest   ★★★★★ Best

Typical

The light from nineteen 2-ft high path lights with 25-W A-lamps mottles the sidewalk leading to the 14-ft high main entrance canopy. The entrance is lighted by four 150-W A-lamps, each in a recessed incandescent downlight. One cobrahead with a 250-W high pressure sodium lamp on a 35-ft pole on the main street does little to light the parking lot or sides of the building.

• INC/25W   ▪ INC/150W   ⬤ HPS/250W

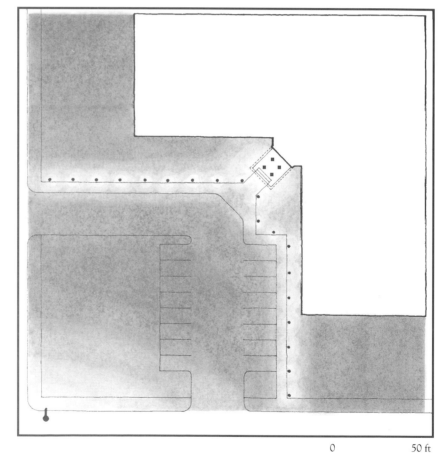

0   50 ft

Sense of Security	Appearance	Initial Equipment Cost	Annual Cost		Average Horizontal Illuminance	Connected Load
			Maintenance	Energy		
★	★★	—	$930	$470	0.17 fc	1100 W

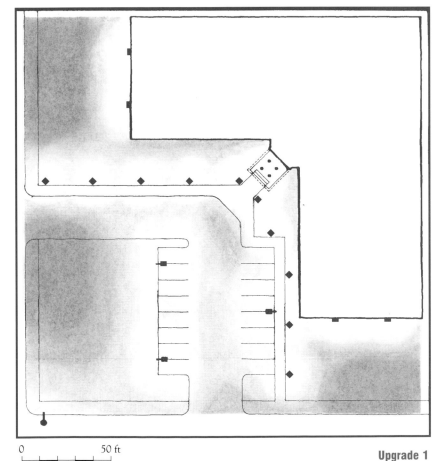

0 50 ft

Upgrade 1

Ten 3¹/₂-ft high bollards with 35-W high pressure sodium lamps improve the uniformity along the sidewalks and make nine of the original sidewalk locations unnecessary. The parking lot lighting is improved by three type III cutoffs with 150-W high pressure sodium lamps on 25-ft poles. Four recessed CFL downlights with 32-W compact fluorescent lamps and low-temperature electronic ballasts replace the luminaires in the ceiling of the entrance canopy. Four downlight wall luminaires with 35-W high pressure sodium lamps light the sides of the building, revealing anyone who might be hiding there. The cobrahead street light remains unchanged.

Upgrade 2

Thirty-two-watt compact fluorescent lamps with low-temperature electronic ballasts replace the 35-W high pressure sodium lamps in the 3¹/₂-ft high bollards and the downlight wall luminaires. In the type III cutoffs, 150-W metal halide lamps replace the high pressure sodium lamps. These lamp changes, along with the 32-W compact fluorescent lamps housed in the CFL downlights, improve the color appearance of the entire site. The cobrahead streetlight remains unchanged.

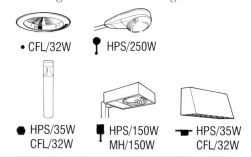

Upgrade 1
Upgrade 2

	Sense of Security	Appearance	Initial Equipment Cost	Annual Cost		Average Horizontal Illuminance	Connected Load
				Maintenance	Energy		
Upgrade 1	★★★	★★	$10,000	$230	$630	1.1 fc	1400 W
Upgrade 2	★★★	★★★	$10,000	$340	$520	1.0 fc	1200 W

Redesign

Twelve 100-W metal halide lamps, each in a decorative cutoff on a 10-ft pole, eliminate many of the dark places on the sidewalk, the parking lot, and the street sidewalk near the sides of the building. Since the ceiling of the entry canopy is painted a light color, a pendant uplight with a 250-W metal halide lamp provides adequate indirect light with minimum glare for the entrance. The cobraheads on the street remain unchanged.

 • MH/100W   ■ MH/250W   ⬤ HPS/250W

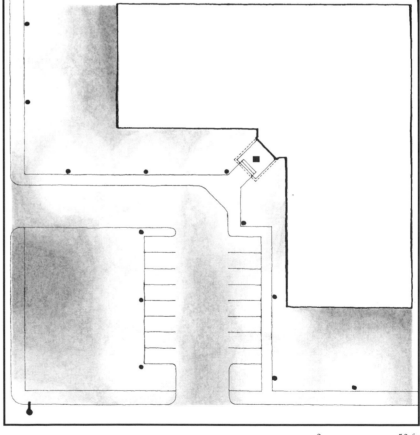

0   50 ft

Sense of Security	Appearance	Initial Equipment Cost	Annual Cost		Average Horizontal Illuminance	Connected Load
			Maintenance	Energy		
★★★★	★★★★	$14,000	$330	$790	1.3 fc	1800 W

MID-RISE APARTMENTS 1

*R*esidents and others approach the entrances to these mid-rise apartment buildings directly from the sidewalk or through a courtyard that opens to the city's streets.

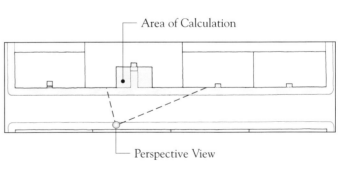

Area of Calculation

Perspective View

	Sense of Security	Appearance	Initial Equipment Cost	Annual Cost	
				Maintenance	Energy
Typical (p. 134)	★	★★	—	$340	$180
Upgrade 1 (p. 135)	★★★★	★★★	$5300	$200	$700
Upgrade 2 (p. 135)	★★★★	★★★★	$5400	$360	$680
Redesign (p. 136)	★★★★	★★★★	$6800	$410	$570

Key: ★ Poorest ★★★★★ Best

Typical

The city or utility company provides three cobrahead street lights with 250-W high pressure sodium lamps mounted on 35-ft poles. A total of seven decorative surface luminaires on the walls and ceilings, each housing a 60-W A-lamp, mark the 8-ft high entrances to the four buildings. Pedestrians sense that the shadows and the hedges could conceal criminals.

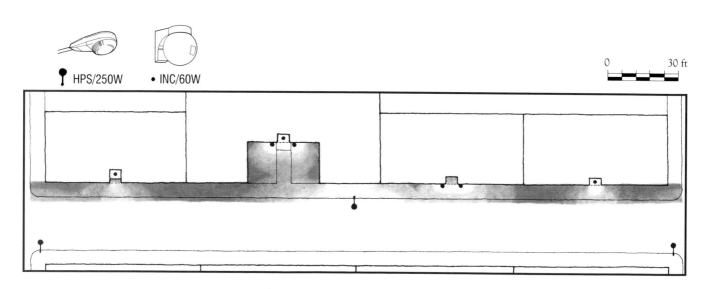

HPS/250W   • INC/60W

0   30 ft

Sense of Security	Appearance	Initial Equipment Cost	Annual Cost		Average Horizontal Illuminance	Connected Load
			Maintenance	Energy		
★	★★	—	$340	$180	0.78 fc	420 W

Upgrade 1

Two performance post tops, mounted on bracket arms to the building's walls, house 70-W high pressure sodium lamps that replace the two decorative surface luminaires at the courtyard building's entrance. Eight more performance post tops with 100-W high pressure sodium lamps mounted to the walls at 13 ft supplement the sidewalk lighting. In the courtyard, light from two performance post tops with 100-W high pressure sodium lamps mounted on 13-ft posts eliminates the shadows. Five 23-W screwbase compact fluorescent lamps replace the A-lamps in the remaining decorative surface luminaires. The cobrahead street lights remain unchanged.

Upgrade 2

The neighborhood benefits from the improved color rendering quality of 70- and 100-W metal halide lamps that replace the high pressure sodium lamps in the 12 performance post tops.

Upgrade 1   ↓ HPS/70,100W   ● HPS/250W   • CFL/23W
Upgrade 2   MH/70,100W

0   30 ft

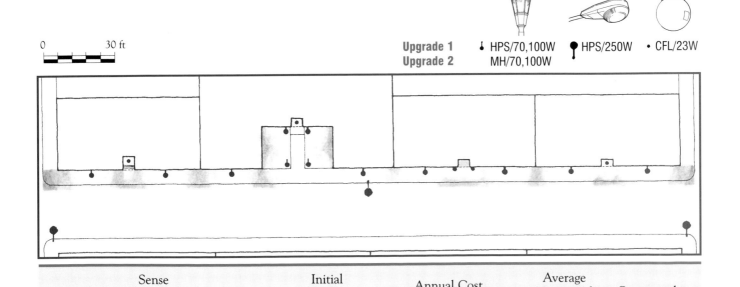

	Sense of Security	Appearance	Initial Equipment Cost	Annual Cost		Average Horizontal Illuminance	Connected Load
				Maintenance	Energy		
Upgrade 1	★★★★	★★★	$5300	$200	$700	2.5 fc	1600 W
Upgrade 2	★★★★	★★★★	$5400	$360	$680	2.4 fc	1600 W

Redesign

Eight downlight wall luminaires mounted 13-ft high on the buildings supplement the street lighting from the existing cobraheads. The downlight wall luminaires each house a 70-W metal halide lamp. At the building entrances, five decorative surface luminaires with 28-W dedicated compact fluorescent lamps are mounted on the walls or ceilings. Four decorative cutoffs with 70-W metal halide lamps mounted on 13-ft poles provide an attractive alternative method of eliminating the shadows of the hedges.

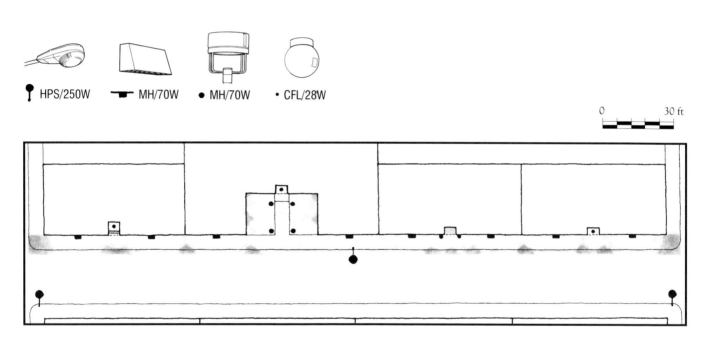

HPS/250W   MH/70W   ● MH/70W   · CFL/28W

0   30 ft

Sense of Security	Appearance	Initial Equipment Cost	Annual Cost		Average Horizontal Illuminance	Connected Load
			Maintenance	Energy		
★★★★	★★★★	$6800	$410	$570	3.6 fc	1300 W

Mid-Rise Apartments 2

*T*he residents of this mid-rise apartment building arrive from a nearby bus stop or from off-street parking near the entrance driveway. Shrubs and trees decorate the building's edges.

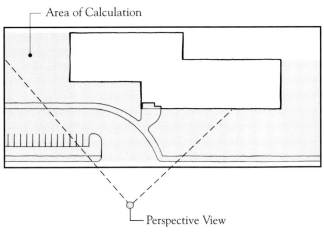

Area of Calculation

Perspective View

	Sense of Security	Appearance	Initial Equipment Cost	Annual Cost	
				Maintenance	Energy
Typical (p. 138)	★	★	—	$220	$390
Upgrade 1 (p. 139)	★★★	★★	$8400	$220	$830
Upgrade 2 (p. 139)	★★★	★★★	$8400	$510	$930
Redesign (p. 140)	★★★★	★★★★	$15,000	$540	$1200

Key: ★ Poorest ★★★★★ Best

Typical

Two cobraheads with 250-W high pressure sodium lamps on a 30-ft pole light only a portion of the parking lot and entrance drive. Dark areas around the building and under the trees provide hiding spots. Two incandescent downlights with 150-W A-lamps recessed in the 12-ft ceiling light the entry.

 HPS/250W   INC/150W

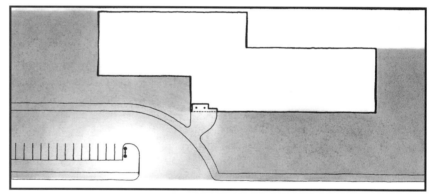

0 ⊢——————⊣ 75 ft

Sense of Security	Appearance	Initial Equipment Cost	Annual Cost		Average Horizontal Illuminance	Connected Load
			Maintenance	Energy		
★	★	—	$220	$390	0.41 fc	900 W

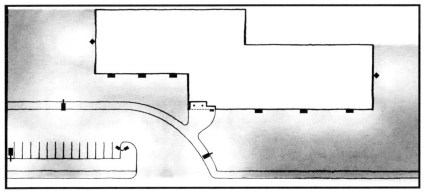

0 ⊢ ⊣ ⊢ ⊣ 75 ft

Upgrade 1

Five type III cutoffs with 150-W high pressure sodium lamps improve the lighting of the parking lot and driveway. Two of these cutoffs are mounted on the existing pole, the other three on new 30-ft poles. Two HID downlights with 50-W metal halide lamps replace the entry downlights. Seven downlight wall luminaires with 50-W high pressure sodium lamps mounted 14-ft high on the wall provide lighting along the the front facade. Two forward-throw performance wall packs with 150-W high pressure sodium lamps, also mounted 14-ft high on the wall, provide lighting along the sides of the building.

Upgrade 2

Changing to metal halide lamps from high pressure sodium provides better color rendering, although high pressure sodium lamps will display red brick fairly well. Here 175-W metal halide lamps replace the 150-W high pressure sodium lamps in the type III cutoffs, 50-W metal halide lamps replace the 50-W high pressure sodium lamps in the downlight wall luminaires, and 175-W metal halide lamps replace the 150-W high pressure sodium lamps in the forward-throw performance wall packs.

Upgrade 1	▮ HPS/150W ▼HPS/50W ◆HPS/150W • MH/50W
Upgrade 2	MH/175W MH/50W MH/175W

	Sense of Security	Appearance	Initial Equipment Cost	Annual Cost		Average Horizontal Illuminance	Connected Load
				Maintenance	Energy		
Upgrade 1	★★★	★★	$8400	$220	$830	0.87 fc	1900 W
Upgrade 2	★★★	★★★	$8400	$510	$930	0.76 fc	2100 W

Redesign

Eighteen performance post tops with 100-W metal halide lamps light the grounds and improve uniformity, creating a park-like atmosphere in the front lawn. Seven of the post tops are wall-bracketed versions mounted at 10-ft, and 11 line the driveway and sidewalk atop 10-ft poles. Two type III cutoff luminaires with 175-W metal halide lamps on 25-ft poles complete the parking lot lighting. Two HID downlights with 50-W metal halide lamps light the entry.

● MH/100W   ▮ MH/175W   • MH/50W

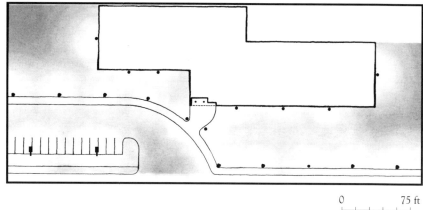

0 ▭▬▭▬ 75 ft

Sense of Security	Appearance	Initial Equipment Cost	Annual Cost		Average Horizontal Illuminance	Connected Load
			Maintenance	Energy		
★★★★	★★★★	$15,000	$540	$1200	0.85 fc	2800 W

GARDEN APARTMENTS

*T*his garden apartment complex includes walks that lead to every destination, but residents often prefer to take shortcuts across the lawns.

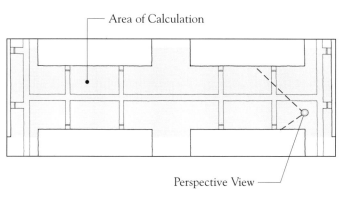

Area of Calculation

Perspective View

	Sense of Security	Appearance	Initial Equipment Cost	Annual Cost	
				Maintenance	Energy
Typical (p. 142)	★	★	—	$610	$840
Upgrade (p. 143)	★★★	★★★	$5000	$360	$1300
Redesign (p. 144)	★★★★	★★★★	$8300	$340	$1000

Key: ★ Poorest ★★★★★ Best

Typical

Between the buildings, six yard lights with 175-W mercury lamps mounted 22-ft high on the gables produce a lot of glare but not enough light for people walking in the dark areas of the court-yards and under the trees. Decorative surface luminaires with 60-W A-lamps mark each of the 12 entrances.

 MV/175W   • INC/60W

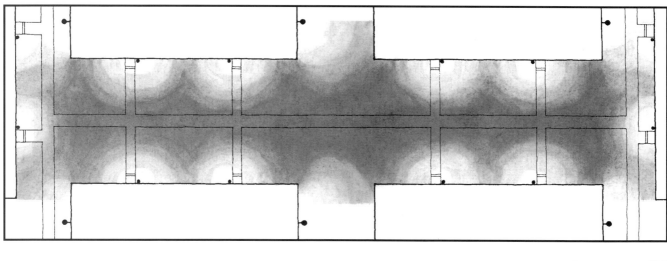

0   50 ft

Sense of Security	Appearance	Initial Equipment Cost	Annual Cost		Average Horizontal Illuminance	Connected Load
			Maintenance	Energy		
★	★	—	$610	$840	0.15 fc	1900 W

Upgrade

Six side-throw performance wall packs with 150-W high pressure sodium lamps replace the yard lights mounted on the gables; another six are mounted 15-ft high on the center of each building. Along with the 12 wall packs, four performance post tops with 70-W high pressure sodium lamps on 8-ft poles decrease the shadows along the central walkway. Twelve 23-W screwbase compact fluorescent lamps fit into the existing decorative surface luminaires by the entrances.

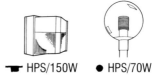

☛ HPS/150W   ● HPS/70W   · CFL/23W

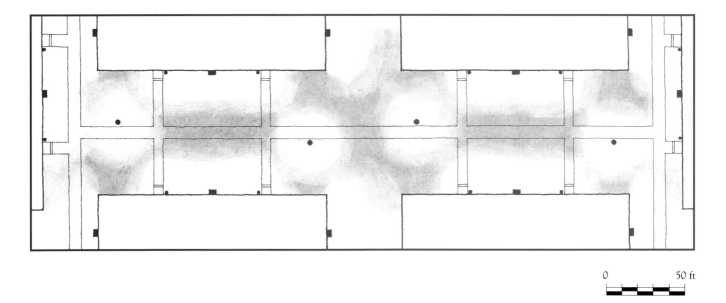

0   50 ft

Sense of Security	Appearance	Initial Equipment Cost	Annual Cost		Average Horizontal Illuminance	Connected Load
			Maintenance	Energy		
★★★	★★★	$5000	$360	$1300	0.98 fc	2900 W

Redesign

Ten performance post tops with 150-W metal halide lamps light the courtyard from 12-ft poles. The luminaire and lamp improves color in the courtyard and raises light levels and uniformity while reducing glare and operating costs. Decorative surface luminaires with dedicated 28-W compact fluorescent lamps mark the entrances.

● MH/150W   • CFL/28W

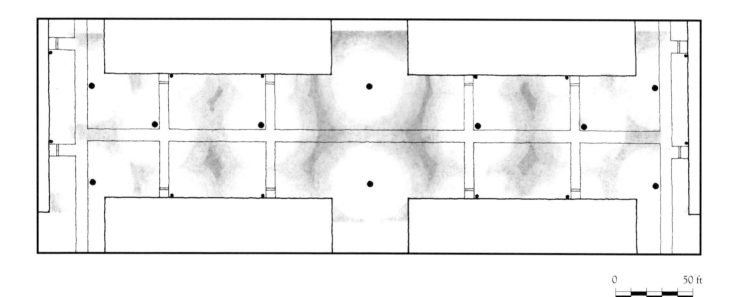

0   50 ft

Sense of Security	Appearance	Initial Equipment Cost	Annual Cost		Average Horizontal Illuminance	Connected Load
			Maintenance	Energy		
★★★★	★★★★	$8300	$340	$1000	1.4 fc	2300 W

HIGH-RISE APARTMENTS

*P*eople walk through courtyards of this complex to the building entrances.

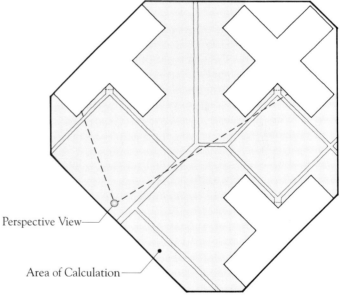

Perspective View

Area of Calculation

	Sense of Security	Appearance	Initial Equipment Cost	Annual Cost	
				Maintenance	Energy
Typical (p. 146)	★	★	—	$730	$2000
Upgrade (p. 147)	★★★	★★	$5400	$340	$5400
Redesign 1 (p. 148)	★★★★	★★★	$34,000	$340	$4400
Redesign 2 (p. 149)	★★★	★★★★	$50,000	$910	$3300

Key: ★ Poorest   ★★★★★ Best

Typical

The three 10-ft high entrance canopies each have two incandescent downlights with 150-W A-lamps. Twelve flood lights with 250-W high pressure sodium lamps mounted 25-ft high on the buildings light only portions of the courtyards.

• INC/150W   🔲 HPS/250W

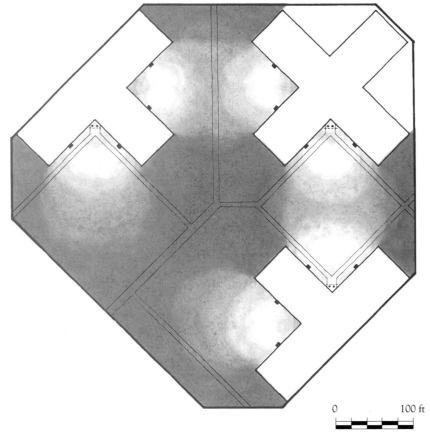

0   100 ft

Sense of Security	Appearance	Initial Equipment Cost	Annual Cost		Average Horizontal Illuminance	Connected Load
			Maintenance	Energy		
★	★	—	$730	$2000	0.91 fc	4500 W

Upgrade

Two decorative surface luminaires with 28-W dedicated compact fluorescent lamps replace the incandescent downlights on the ceilings of the three entrance canopies. Eleven sports flood lights, mounted 130-ft high on the roofs, replace the existing flood lights, improve coverage, and reduce glare. Each of the sports flood lights houses a 1000-W high pressure sodium lamp. Maintenance personnel must aim these sports flood lights carefully to minimize glare and replace burned out lamps quickly to minimize dark spots.

- CFL/28W   ▼ HPS/1000W

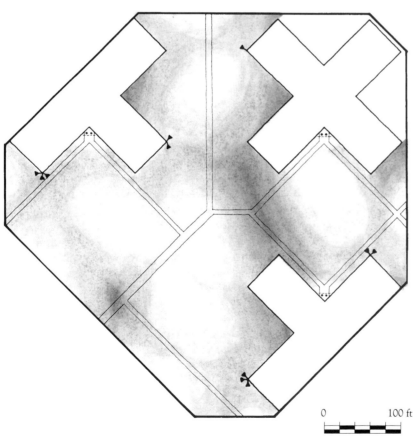

0   100 ft

Sense of Security	Appearance	Initial Equipment Cost	Annual Cost		Average Horizontal Illuminance	Connected Load
			Maintenance	Energy		
★★★	★★	$5400	$340	$5400	1.6 fc	12,000 W

Redesign 1

The ceilings of each of the three entrance canopies provide suitable locations for two decorative surface luminaires, each housing a 28-W dedicated compact fluorescent lamp. The courtyard receives light from 21 type V cutoffs with 400-W high pressure sodium lamps mounted three each on 50-ft poles located about 150 ft apart. Light levels and uniformity tend to drop around the perimeter of the complex unless supplemented by lighting from perimeter sources, such as street lights.

 CFL/28W    HPS/400W

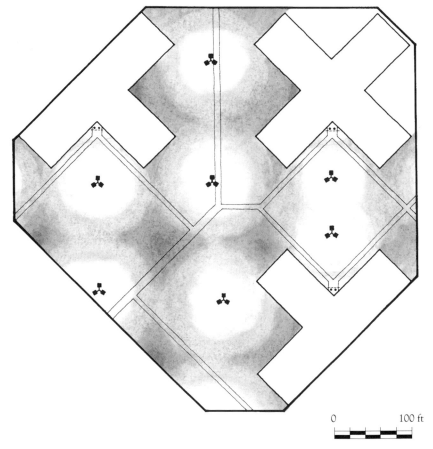

0   100 ft

Sense of Security	Appearance	Initial Equipment Cost	Annual Cost		Average Horizontal Illuminance	Connected Load
			Maintenance	Energy		
★★★★	★★★	$34,000	$340	$4400	3.0 fc	10,000 W

Redesign 2

When vandalism is not a concern, a large complex can appear park-like; 29 decorative cutoffs on 12-ft poles provide light along the walkways and into the courtyards using 100-W metal halide lamps. Four 50-ft poles, each with two type V cutoffs that house a 400-W high pressure sodium lamp, provide light farther from the walkways. The three entrances are each lighted by two decorative surface luminaires with 28-W dedicated compact fluorescent lamps on the canopy ceilings.

● MH/100W   ▮ HPS/400W   · CFL/28W

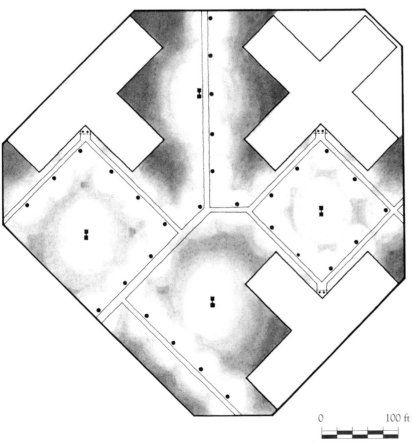

0   100 ft

Sense of Security	Appearance	Initial Equipment Cost	Annual Cost		Average Horizontal Illuminance	Connected Load
			Maintenance	Energy		
★★★	★★★★	$50,000	$910	$3300	1.9 fc	7500 W

ALLEY

G arages, fenced yards, back doors, and service entrances face this residential alley. Residents sometimes carry their trash out at night, keeping a wary eye out for transients who use the alley as a shortcut.

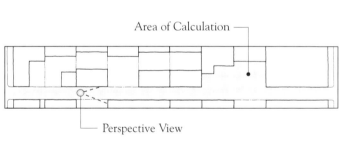

Area of Calculation

Perspective View

	Sense of Security	Appearance	Initial Equipment Cost	Annual Cost	
				Maintenance	Energy
Typical (p. 152)	★	★	—	$45	$310
Redesign 1 (p. 153)	★★★	★★	$1900	$89	$370
Redesign 2 (p. 154)	★★★	★★	$5800	$72	$340

Key: ★ Poorest ★★★★★ Best

Typical

The few pools of light seem only to heighten people's apprehension. Light from the 175-W mercury vapor lamp in each of the two yard lights and the two-headed 150-W PAR lamp holder over one garage does not light the alley brightly enough or eliminate the dark hiding spots. Glare from these sources makes it hard for residents to identify even familiar faces.

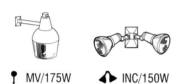

 MV/175W   INC/150W

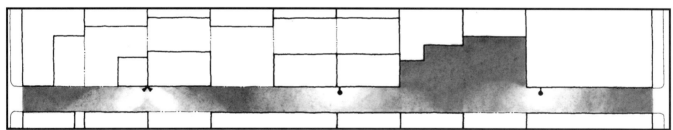

0   50 ft

Sense of Security	Appearance	Initial Equipment Cost	Annual Cost		Average Horizontal Illuminance	Connected Load
			Maintenance	Energy		
★	★	—	$45	$310	0.54 fc	700 W

Redesign 1

The neighborhood association installs nine shielded wall packs with 70-W high pressure sodium lamps mounted 10-ft high on the buildings. One of these wall packs lights the recess off the alley.

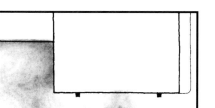

■ HPS/70W

0   50 ft

Sense of Security	Appearance	Initial Equipment Cost	Annual Cost		Average Horizontal Illuminance	Connected Load
			Maintenance	Energy		
★★★	★★	$1900	$89	$370	1.4 fc	860 W

Redesign 2

The city or utility, perhaps in response to a neighborhood request, installs six cobraheads with 100-W high pressure sodium lamps on 20-ft poles. Two of the cobraheads are aimed to direct light into a potential hiding place, the recess off the alley.

HPS/100W

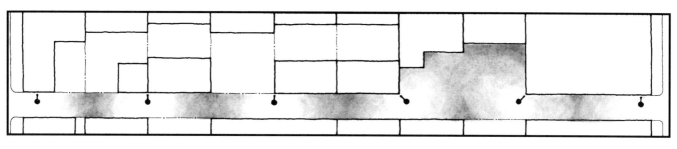

0   50 ft

Sense of Security	Appearance	Initial Equipment Cost	Annual Cost		Average Horizontal Illuminance	Connected Load
			Maintenance	Energy		
★★★	★★	$5800	$72	$340	1.7 fc	780 W

ECONOMICS

Each of the outdoor lighting patterns varies in cost. This chapter provides forms and tables to use when analyzing the equipment, energy, and maintenance costs of design alternatives. The worksheet was used to analyze the costs of equipment and the cost of operating the designs presented in *The Outdoor Lighting Pattern Book* and is useful as a way to make preliminary estimates of the costs of other designs.

The luminaire table (p. 159) includes prices for the typical luminaires described in the luminaire chapter

Table of Contents

and used in the designs in this book. The lamp tables (pp. 160–162) give information about lamps used typically in outdoor lighting designs. In addition to price, input power, and lamp life, the tables list light output and color characteristics to allow easy comparison of the lamp options. The pole and control tables (p. 163) list prices for poles and controls.

To estimate the initial cost of equipment in a lighting design, complete worksheet lines A through O. O represents a rough estimate of the initial cost of equipment including luminaires, ballasts, lamps, controls, and poles used in the design.

To estimate the annual costs of operating the design, complete worksheet items P through AA. V represents a rough estimate of the annual cost incurred for maintaining the equipment used in the design, including the cost of buying new lamps and the cost of labor for relamping a luminaire. Z is the annual energy cost. AA combines the maintenance and energy costs.

The worksheet and detailed directions for each line of the worksheet appear on the following pages.

Economics Worksheet

Design Name: _____
Version: _____

		Luminaire Type 1	Luminaire Type 2	Luminaire Type 3	Total
Initial Costs					
A.	Luminaire Name				
B.	Lamp Type				
C.	Number of Luminaires				
D.	Cost per Luminaire (p. 159)	$	$	$	
E.	Total Luminaire Cost (C × D)	$	$	$	
F.	Lamps per Luminaire				
G.	Total Number of Lamps (C × F)				
H.	Lamp Cost (pp. 160–162)	$	$	$	
I.	Total Lamp Cost (G × H)	$	$	$	
J.	Number of Poles				
K.	Pole Cost (p. 163)	$	$	$	
L.	Total Pole Cost (J × K)	$	$	$	
M.	Control System Cost (p. 163)	$	$	$	
N.	Incentives or Discounts	$	$	$	
O.	**Total Equipment Cost E+I+L+M−N**	$	$	$	$
Annual Costs					
P.	Average Daily Use	_____ (hrs)	_____ (hrs)	_____ (hrs)	
Q.	Operating Time (365 × P)	_____ (hrs)	_____ (hrs)	_____ (hrs)	
R.	Average Rated Lamp Life (pp. 160–162)	_____ (hrs)	_____ (hrs)	_____ (hrs)	
S.	Lamps Used (G × Q/R)				
T.	Relamping Labor (p. 159)	$	$	$	
U.	Lamp Replacement Cost (H + T)	$	$	$	
V.	Maintenance Cost (S × U)	$	$	$	
W.	Input Power (pp. 160–162)	_____ (W)	_____ (W)	_____ (W)	
X.	Energy Use (G × W × Q/1000)	_____ (kWh)	_____ (kWh)	_____ (kWh)	
Y.	Electricity Cost	_____ ($/kWh)	_____ ($/kWh)	_____ ($/kWh)	
Z.	Annual Energy Cost (X × Y)	$	$	$	
AA.	**Annual Operating Cost (V + Z)**	$	$	$	$

Instructions

A. Enter the names of the luminaire types used in the design and complete one column for each. The total column sums the costs for all the luminaire types in the design. If you have not selected a specific luminaire, use the generic luminaire types listed in the luminaire table and described in the luminaire chapter.

B. Enter the type of lamp to be used in the luminaire. The luminaire chapter lists lamps typically used in each luminaire.

C. Count the number of luminaires of each type used in the design. A lighting plan, if you have one, can help. If not, the designs in *The Outdoor Lighting Pattern Book* can help you estimate the proper spacing of luminaires for your design.

D. Enter the price of one luminaire. For luminaires for HID and fluorescent lamps, this price typically includes the ballast. If the luminaire has an integral photosensor, add its price to the price of the luminaire. A distributor or contractor can provide price quotes for the luminaire you have selected, including any applicable discounts for quantity. The luminaire table provides typical price ranges for each luminaire type and the cost used in the evaluations of the designs in *The Outdoor Lighting Pattern Book*.

E. Multiply C by D to get the cost of the luminaires.

F. Enter the number of lamps used in each luminaire. Most outdoor HID luminaires operate only one lamp.

G. Multiply C by F to get the total number of lamps used by each luminaire type.

H. Enter the cost of one lamp. Use price quotes from a distributor or contractor or use the values listed in the lamp tables (pp. 160–162). The values are the ones used to evaluate the designs in *The Outdoor Lighting Pattern Book*.

I. Multiply G by H to get the total cost of lamps for this luminaire type.

J. Count the number of poles used in the design for each luminaire type. Use the lighting plan, if you have one. If not, the designs in *The Outdoor Lighting Pattern Book* can help you estimate the spacing and number of poles in your design.

K. Enter the cost of one pole, adding to it the cost for the number of arms indicated on the lighting plan. Use price quotes from a distributor or contractor or use the values listed in the pole table (p. 163).

L. Multiply J by K to get the total cost of poles for each luminaire type.

M. Use the table on page 163 to estimate the cost of the control system(s) operating the luminaires. If the luminaires are controlled only by integral photosensors, the cost of the control is included with the cost of the luminaire in line D.

N. Enter the total amount of any incentive or discount, if available. Some electric utilities offer discounts, rebates, promotions, or other incentives to reduce the cost of outdoor lighting equipment.

O. Add E, I, L, and M, then subtract N to get the total initial cost of equipment. Installation and wiring are not included because they depend on the existing electrical locations and site-specific parameters. Consult with your engineer and contractor for the installation and wiring costs. For quick planning, double the equipment cost to get a rough estimate of the total initial cost.

P. Estimate the average hours of one lamp's operation per day. Consider the impact of photocells or time clocks in your estimate. If the lamp is operated by a photocell, estimate 12 hours per day.

Q. Multiply P by 365 days to get the annual hours of lamp operation.

R. Look up the average rated lamp life in the lamp table (pp. 160–162) or in a manufacturer's catalog. A fluorescent lamp that operates for long hours without being switched may last longer than the rated life. For example, a fluorescent lamp operating 12 hours per start may operate 50 percent longer than its average rated life. HID and fluorescent lamps that are switched frequently may not operate as long as the average rated lamp life.

S. Multiply G by Q, then divide by R to determine the average number of lamps that need to be replaced in a year.

T. For lamps replaced by hired labor, use the luminaire table (p. 159) to find the cost of labor for replacing the lamp or lamps in one luminaire.

U. Add H and T to get the lamp replacement cost, which includes the cost of replacement lamps and the labor of relamping.

V. Multiply S by U to get the annual maintenance cost.

W. Enter the input power of one lamp, including the ballast. The lamp table (pp. 160–162) gives default values for common lamp types which include the ballast power. Input power will vary with ballast manufacturer, type of ballast, and the number of lamps that are operated per ballast. For more accurate estimates, consult manufacturers' data and the sources listed under Further Reading (p. 206).

X. Multiply G by W by Q, then divide by 1000 to get the annual energy use in kilowatt hours.

Y. Enter the average cost of electricity in your area. Electricity costs in North America range from $0.03 to more than $0.18 per kWh. *The Outdoor Lighting Pattern Book* costs have been calculated using $0.10 per kWh. Some utilities have off-peak rates and demand charges that should be considered in determining an average rate per kWh.

Z. Multiply X by Y to get the annual cost of energy.

AA. Add V and Z to get total annual costs of operating a design including the costs of energy and of buying and replacing lamps.

Luminaire Table			
Luminaire	Generic Price ($)	Price Range ($)	Relamping Labor ($)
Bollard	360	200 – 500	10
Canopy Light	170	150 – 300	15
CFL Downlight	200	150 – 250	15
CFL Wall Pack*	75	70 – 120	10
Cobrahead*	210	170 – 320	23
Decorative Cutoff*	720	520 –1000	23
Decorative Post Top*	170	120 – 320	15
Decorative Surface Luminaire*	75	50 – 100	10
Downlight Wall Luminaire*	320	170 – 420	10
Enclosed Fluorescent Strip (4 ft)	90	75 – 120	15
Enclosed Fluorescent Strip (8 ft)	120	100 – 150	15
Flood or Sports Flood Light*	320	220 – 820	15
Fluorescent Sign Lighter (4 and 8 ft)	200	150 – 250	15
Garage Luminaire	250	200 – 500	15
Halogen Flood Light*	45	40 – 70	15
HID Downlight	200	150 – 250	15
Incandescent Downlight	70	50 – 150	15
Open Fluorescent Strip (4 ft)	30	20 – 40	10
Open Fluorescent Strip (8 ft)	50	35 – 55	10
PAR Lamp Holder*	40	35 – 65	10
Path Light	70	25 – 200	10
Pendant Uplight	300	250 – 500	15
Performance Post Top*	270	220 – 520	15
Performance Wall Pack*	160	120 – 320	15
Refractor Basket	150	100 – 200	15
Shielded Wall Pack*	170	120 – 195	15
Type III Cutoff*	320	270 – 420	23
Type V Cutoff*	550	470 – 720	23
Wall Pack*	100	70 – 120	15
Yard Light*	50	40 – 95	15

* Prices include $20 for an integral photosensor.

HID Lamp Table

Power Rated (W)	Power Input (W)	Lamp Life (hr)	Light Output (lumens [lm])	CCT (K)	CRI	Efficacy (lm/W)	Typical Price ($)
Metal Halide Lamps							
50	69	5000 – 10,000	2800 – 3500	3000 – 4000	65 – 70	56 – 70	46
70	95	5000 – 15,000	4800 – 5200	3000 – 4300	65 – 75	69 – 74	50
100	125	10,000 – 15,000	7800 – 8500	3000 – 4300	65 – 80	78 – 85	50
150	190	15,000	12,500 – 14,250	3000 – 4000	65 – 75	83 – 95	58
175	215	7500 – 10,000	12,000 – 15,000	3400 – 4400	65 – 70	69 – 86	38
250	295	10,000	19,800 – 20,500	3700 – 4000	65 – 70	79 – 82	43
400	458	20,000	36,000	3700 – 4000	65 – 70	90	41
1000	1080	12,000	110,000	3400 – 4000	65 – 70	110	94
High Pressure Sodium Lamps							
35	53	16,000+ – 24,000+	2150 – 2250	1900 – 2100	20 – 22	61 – 64	39
50	64	24,000+	3800 – 4000	1900 – 2100	21 – 22	76 – 80	39
70	95	24,000+	5860 – 6400	1900 – 2100	21 – 22	85 – 91	39
100	130	24,000+	8800 – 9500	2000 – 2100	21 – 22	88 – 93	43
150	188	24,000+	15,000 – 16,000	2000 – 2100	21 – 22	100– 107	46
250	300	24,000+	26,000 – 29,000	2100	21 – 22	104 – 110	54
400	465	24,000+	47,500 – 51,000	2100	21 – 22	119 – 125	50
1000	1100	24,000+	140,000	2100	21 – 22	140	123
Mercury Vapor Lamps							
75	93	16,000 – 24,000+	2800 – 3150	3200 – 4000	45 – 50	37 – 42	40
100	125	18,000 – 24,000+	3850 – 4400	2800 – 7000	15 – 50	39 – 44	26
175	200	24,000+	7900 – 8500	3700 – 6800	15 – 50	45 – 49	17
400	455	24,000+	21,500 – 22,500	3700 – 6800	15 – 50	54 – 56	25

Fluorescent Lamp Table

Lamp Type	Power Rated (W)	Input (W)	Lamp Life (hr)	Light Output (lumens [lm])	CCT (K)	CRI	Efficacy (lm/W)	Typical Price ($)
T12 and T8 Lamps								
4-ft T12/Cool White*	40	46**	20,000+	3050	4150	62	76	2.50
4-ft T12/RE741	40	46**	20,000+	3200	4100	70	80	4.50
4-ft T12 HO/Cool White	60	72**	12,000	4050 – 4100	4100 – 4200	62	68	9
4-ft T12 HO/RE741	60	72**	12,000	4250	4100	70	71	11
8-ft Slimline/Cool White*	75	90**	12,000	6100 – 6500	4100 – 4200	62	81 – 87	10
8-ft Slimline/RE741	75	90**	12,000	6425	4100	70	86	12
8-ft T12 HO/Cool White*	110	128**	12,000	8800 – 8900	4100 – 4200	62	80 – 81	6
8-ft T12 HO/RE741	110	128**	12,000	9200	4100	70	84	12
4-ft T8/RE741	32	34	20,000	2850	4100	75	89	4
8-ft T8/RE741	59/60	68**	15,000	4500 – 5800	4100	75	76 – 98	8
Compact Fluorescent Lamps								
Triple Tube	18	18	10,000	1120 – 1200	2700 – 4100	82	62 – 67	23
Triple Tube	26	27	10,000	1610 – 1800	2700 – 4100	82	62 – 69	23
Triple Tube	32	34	10,000	2200 – 2400	2700 – 4100	82	69 – 75	23
Quad Tube	18 – 20	20 – 22	10,000	1200 – 1250	2700 – 4100	82 – 85	60 – 69	13
Quad Tube	26 – 28	30 – 32	10,000	1600 – 1800	2700 – 5000	82 – 85	57 – 69	14
Screwbase Compact Fluorescent-Electronic								
Triple Tube with Capsule	18	18	10,000	1100	2700	82	61	21
Triple and Quad Tube	20	20	10,000	1200	2700	82	60	25
Triple Tube	23	23	10,000	1550	2700	82	67	26

* Production and import prohibited by EPACT.
** Input power using low-temperature ballasts. Input power for standard ballasts will be lower.

Incandescent Lamp Table								
	Power							
Lamp Type	Rated (W)	Input (W)	Lamp Life (hr)	Light Output (lumens [lm])	CCT (K)	CRI	Efficacy (lm/W)	Typical Price ($)
Tubular Halogen								
Tubular	100	100	1500 – 2000	1650	2950	95+	17	12
Tubular	300	300	2000	6000	3050	95+	30	16
Tubular	500	500	2000	10,500 – 11,100	3050	95+	21 – 22	11
Tubular	1000	1000	2000 – 3000	21,000 – 21,500	3050	95+	21 – 22	45
Tubular IR	350	350	2000	10,000	3050	95+	29	17
Tubular IR	900	900	2000	32,000	3050	95+	36	46
Reflector								
PAR38*	150	150	2000	1740	2800	95+	12	7.50
PAR38 Halogen	90	90	2000 – 2500	1270 – 1300	2900	95+	14	10
PAR38 Halogen	120	120	3000	1900	2900	95+	16	12
PAR38 Halogen*	150	150	3000 – 4000	1725 – 2200	2900	95+	12 – 15	16
PAR38 Halogen IR	60	60	3000	1110	2825	95+	19	15
PAR38 Halogen IR	100	100	3000	2000	2925	95+	20	14
A-line Incandescent								
A19	25	25	1000 – 2500	215 – 375	2800	95+	9 – 15	1.50
A19	40	40	1000 – 1500	460 – 495	2800	95+	12	1
A19	60	60	1000	860 – 890	2800	95+	14 – 15	1
A19	100	100	750	1720 – 1750	2800	95+	17 – 18	0.75
A21	150	150	750	2850	2800	95+	19	1.50
Halogen	42	42	3,500	570	3050	95+	14	3
Halogen	50 – 52	50 – 52	2000 – 3500	770 – 830	3050	95+	15 – 17	4.50
Halogen	90 – 100	90 – 100	2000 – 2250	1680 – 1880	3050	95+	19	5

* Production and import of versions with efficacy less than 14.5 prohibited by EPACT

Ever
more
ratin
or su
horiz
T
20,0
M
light
(rest
5 to
A
lumi
the l
the a
for c
minu
oute
tube
shro
S
and
affor
factu
for n
lamp
simil
ate
muc
T
struc
lamp

Rate
(W

50
70
100
150
175
250
400
1000

Pole Table	
Pole Type and Height	Typical Price ($)
Aluminum 8 ft	290
Aluminum 10 ft	350
Aluminum 12 ft	400
Aluminum 15 ft	520
Aluminum 20 ft	640
Aluminum 25 ft	940
Aluminum 30 ft	1200
Aluminum 35 ft	1600
Aluminum 40 ft	1900
Aluminum 50 ft	2800
Steel 8 ft	460
Steel 10 ft	490
Steel 12 ft	510
Steel 15 ft	680
Steel 18 ft	850
Steel 20 ft	900
Steel 25 ft	1100
Steel 30 ft	1300
Steel 35 ft	1400
Steel 40 ft	1500
Steel 45 ft	1600
Steel 50 ft	1800

Arms	
Aluminum	
one arm	75
two arms	100
three arms	150
four arms	190
Steel	
one arm	70
two arms	150
three arms	170
four arms	230

Control Table	
Control	Typical Price ($)
Building-Mounted Photocell	20
Time Clock	60
Motion Sensor	60
Time Clock and Photocell	80

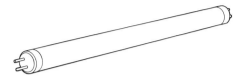

Fluorescent

Some outdoor and security lighting situations require a light source that is inexpensive or starts quickly. For these applications, fluorescent lamps are a good choice.

For many years, when specifiers designated fluorescent lamps for outdoor applications, they chose cool white (CRI of 62, CCT of 4150 K). The U.S. Energy Policy Act of 1992 (EPACT), however, banned the manufacture and import of many of the most common fluorescent lamps, including some cool-white versions, by setting minimum efficacy and CRI requirements. By October 31, 1995, EPACT had excluded from the U.S. market standard-color 40-W F40T12, 75-W F96T12 slimline, and 110-W F96T12 high-output lamps.

Although still available in energy-saving wattages, cool-white lamps have been replaced in many applications by the newer rare-earth (RE) phosphor lamps, available in all T8 and standard and energy-saving T12 wattages. RE lamps offer CRIs from the mid-70s to the mid-80s in three standard CCT values, 3000 K, 3500 K, and 4100 K.

Fluorescent lamps for outdoor lighting include T8 (1-in. diameter) and T12 ($1^1/_2$-in. diameter) rapid-start, slimline, high-output and very-high-output types. The most common lamps for lighting outdoor areas such as canopied walks, building facades, and garages are 4-ft (F40) and 8-ft (F96) T12 rapid-start and slimline lamps, and 4-ft (F32) and 8-ft (F96) T8 lamps. High-output (HO) 4-ft and 8-ft T12 lamps are used in cold climates where rapid-start and slimline lamps may have trouble starting. There are few luminaires for outdoor lighting that accommodate shorter T8 and T12 lamps. The high- and very-high-output lamps are almost exclusively for large internally lighted signs.

T12 and T8 Lamps Commonly Used in Outdoor Applications								
Lamp Type	Power Rated (W)	Input (W)	Lamp Life (hr)	Light Output (lumens [lm])	CCT (K)	CRI	Efficacy (lm/W)	Typical Price ($)
4-ft T12/Cool White*	40	46**	20,000+	3050	4150	62	76	2.50
4-ft T12/RE741	40	46**	20,000+	3200	4100	70	80	4.50
4-ft T12 HO/Cool White	60	72**	12,000	4050 – 4100	4100 – 4200	62	68	9
4-ft T12 HO/RE741	60	72**	12,000	4250	4100	70	71	11
8-ft Slimline/Cool White*	75	90**	12,000	6100 – 6500	4100 – 4200	62	81 – 87	10
8-ft Slimline/RE741	75	90**	12,000	6425	4100	70	86	12
8-ft T12 HO/Cool White*	110	128**	12,000	8800 – 8900	4100 – 4200	62	80 – 81	6
8-ft T12 HO/RE741	110	128**	12,000	9200	4100	70	84	12
4-ft T8/RE741	32	34	20,000	2850	4100	75	89	4
8-ft T8/RE741	59/60	68**	15,000	4500 – 5800	4100	75	76 – 98	8

* Production and import prohibited by EPACT.
** Input power using low-temperature ballasts. Input power for standard ballasts will be lower.

T12 and T8

The 4-ft and 8-ft T8 and T12 lamps have comparable light output and efficacies to similar-wattage metal halide and HPS lamps, but greater than similar-wattage incandescent lamps. Their output diminishes as the lamps and phosphors age and the electrodes deteriorate. Temperature strongly affects light output; a cold fluorescent lamp produces far less than its rated light output, and in extreme cold, rapid-start and slimline versions may not even start. Enclosed luminaires and low-temperature ballasts add reliability for starting these lamps in extremely cold weather. Energy-saving T12 lamps are not designed for use in cold weather and are not recommended for use outdoors, even when enclosed. T8 lamps must be enclosed to operate reliably below 50°F.

The average rated life of the 4-ft energy-saving fluorescent lamp is between 15,000 and 20,000 hours. Slimline and high-output lamps average 12,000 hours life.

Compact Fluorescent

Compact fluorescent lamps, or CFLs, have tube diameters of $^5/_8$ inch (T5) or less and range in length from $4^1/_2$ to 23 inches. In outdoor lighting, luminaires for 6 to 8-inch-long CFLs usually mark entrances and walkways.

CFLs have CRIs in the mid-80s, a product of their rare-earth phosphors, and CCTs of 2700, 3000, 3500, 4100, and 5000 K. CFLs do not have the high efficacies of T8 and T12 lamps, but generally produce more light than incandescent lamps of three times the wattage. CFLs provide light output similar to the 25 to 100-W incandescent lamps they often replace. However, lamp burning position is important; mounting CFLs base up generally yields optimum light output.

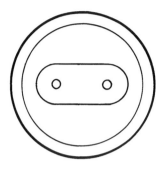

One end of a T12 lamp

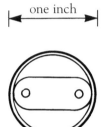

One end of a T8 lamp

	Power							
Lamp Type	Rated (W)	Input (W)	Lamp Life (hr)	Light Output (lumens [lm])	CCT (K)	CRI	Efficacy (lm/W)	Typical Price ($)
Compact Fluorescent Lamps								
Triple Tube	18	18	10,000	1120 – 1200	2700 – 4100	82	62 – 67	23
Triple Tube	26	27	10,000	1610 – 1800	2700 – 4100	82	62 – 69	23
Triple Tube	32	34	10,000	2200 – 2400	2700 – 4100	82	69 – 75	23
Quad Tube	18 – 20	20 – 22	10,000	1200 – 1250	2700 – 4100	82 – 85	60 – 69	13
Quad Tube	26 – 28	30 – 32	10,000	1600 – 1800	2700 – 5000	82 – 85	57 – 69	14
Screwbase Compact Fluorescent-Electronic								
Triple Tube with Capsule	18	18	10,000	1100	2700	82	61	21
Triple and Quad Tube	20	20	10,000	1200	2700	82	60	25
Triple Tube	23	23	10,000	1550	2700	82	67	26

Table caption: **Compact Fluorescent Lamps Commonly Used in Outdoor Applications**

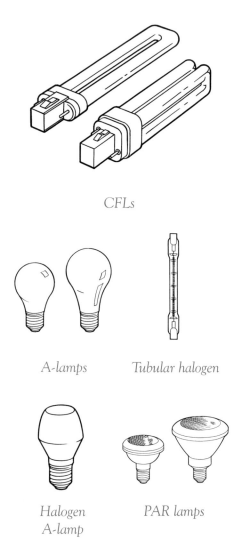

CFLs

A-lamps   Tubular halogen

Halogen   PAR lamps
A-lamp

The dedicated CFL requires a special plug-in socket and a separate ballast in a luminaire designed especially for CFL lamps. The use of dedicated CFLs prevents the easy replacement of burned-out, energy-efficient CFLs with less expensive incandescent lamps. CFLs come in twin-tube, multi-tube, and and other designs.

The light output of CFLs diminishes with age. Temperature also affects the light output of CFLs as it does full-size fluorescent lamps. CFLs need low-temperature ballasts to enable cold temperature starting. Electronic ballasts are particularly good for starting CFLs, especially screwbase types, in cold weather. The average rated life of CFLs is 10,000 hours.

Incandescent

Incandescent lamps continue to appear in outdoor lighting, especially in decorative lanterns and small area flood lighting. The tungsten-halogen family of incandescents such as PARs and IR (infrared)-PARs provide specific beam control, and combine white color with the highest efficacies available in incandescent lamps. Halogen A-lamps provide slightly better efficacy than standard A-lamps. Halogen PARs and halogen IR (infrared) PARs replace standard PAR lamps that were eliminated by the minimum efficacies set by EPACT. Halogen IR technology has also improved the efficacy of certain tubular halogen lamp used in expensive floodlights. Incandescent lamps offer low initial cost, instant full light output, and no temperature restriction. However, incandescents remain as the lowest efficacy and shortest life light source used in outdoor and security lighting.

Incandescent Lamps Commonly Used in Outdoor Applications

Lamp Type	Power Rated (W)	Input (W)	Lamp Life (hr)	Light Output (lumens [lm])	CCT (K)	CRI	Efficacy (lm/W)	Typical Price ($)
Tubular Halogen								
Tubular	100	100	1500 – 2000	1650	2950	95+	17	12
Tubular	300	300	2000	6000	3050	95+	30	16
Tubular	500	500	2000	10,500 – 11,100	3050	95+	21 – 22	11
Tubular	1000	1000	2000 – 3000	21,000 – 21,500	3050	95+	21 – 22	45
Tubular IR	350	350	2000	10,000	3050	95+	29	17
Tubular IR	900	900	2000	32,000	3050	95+	36	46
Reflector								
PAR38*	150	150	2000	1740	2800	95+	12	7.50
PAR38 Halogen	90	90	2000 – 2500	1270 – 1300	2900	95+	14	10
PAR38 Halogen	120	120	3000	1900	2900	95+	16	12
PAR38 Halogen*	150	150	3000 – 4000	1725 – 2200	2900	95+	12 – 15	16
PAR38 Halogen IR	60	60	3000	1110	2825	95+	19	15
PAR38 Halogen IR	100	100	3000	2000	2925	95+	20	14
A-line Incandescent								
A19	25	25	1000 – 2500	215 – 375	2800	95+	9 – 15	1.50
A19	40	40	1000 – 1500	460 – 495	2800	95+	12	1
A19	60	60	1000	860 – 890	2800	95+	14 – 15	1
A19	100	100	750	1720 – 1750	2800	95+	17 – 18	0.75
A21	150	150	750	2850	2800	95+	19	1.50
Halogen	42	42	3,500	570	3050	95+	14	3
Halogen	50 – 52	50 – 52	2000 – 3500	770 – 830	3050	95+	15 – 17	4.50
Halogen	90 – 100	90 – 100	2000 – 2250	1680 – 1880	3050	95+	19	5

* Production and import of versions with efficacy less than 14.5 prohibited by EPACT

LUMINAIRES

A luminaire includes one or more lamps, together with the parts designed to distribute light, to position and protect the lamps, and to connect the lamps to a power supply. A luminaire's most important characteristic is its capacity to distribute light efficiently to desired areas or objects. This section includes drawings and descriptions of 28 generic luminaire types, listed in alphabetical order. This section also

- describes luminaire mounting heights and locations,
- lists lamps suitable for each luminaire,
- describes the lamp's orientation within the luminaire,
- includes each luminaire's size and shape, function, and light distribution capabilities,
- provides location and aiming information and cautions on glare or light trespass, and

- lists luminaires that should be compared for function, cost, light output, mounting, appropriate lamp types, glare, and light distribution.

Manufacturers' catalogs also provide information about components, styles, finishes, mounting configurations and heights, and performance specifications for specific luminaires.

Luminaires also come in different grades of quality. When selecting a luminaire, specifiers should consider whether the manufacturer specializes in residential or commercial luminaires or offers a full product line. See the appendix describing lighting equipment materials for more information about luminaire construction. Also consider how long the manufacturer has been in business, the warranty, the availability of full photometric data and good application information, and the availability of help on wind loading.

Table of Contents

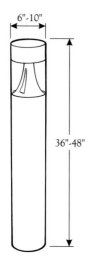

Bollard

Grade mount

Lamps

Metal halide (50, 70, 100, 150, and 175 W)
High pressure sodium (35, 50, 70, 100, and 150 W)
CFL (26 and 32 W)

Lamp Orientation   Vertical

Description ■ A bollard is a metal tube with a luminaire integrated into its top. The luminaire distributes light downward in a circular type V distribution with a diameter about two times the height of the tube. The reflector is usually visible and is often a source of direct glare to passersby.

Application Tips ■ Bollards are generally used as pathmarkers. Because of their mounting height and downlight distribution, they generally do not provide much upward light, making it difficult for people to recognize others. Bollards should not be the only luminaires in an application, rather they should be used as supplements to type III or type V cutoffs or to performance post tops.

Compare ■ Path lights, performance post tops, decorative post tops

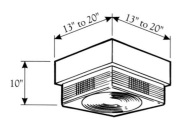

Canopy Light

Surface mount on a canopy or soffit 14 to 20 ft high

Lamps

Metal halide (100, 175, and 250 W)
High pressure sodium (100 and 150 W)

Lamp Orientation   Horizontal or vertical

Description ■ With its dropped prismatic lens, this luminaire effectively lights vertical and horizontal surfaces without undue glare. Manufacturers usually offer optional vandal-resistant lenses.

Application Tips ■ This luminaire suits the canopied sidewalks of retail strip centers because it lights adjacent walls and the faces of pedestrians. However, its size and brightness limit its application to spaces where it can be mounted at least 14-ft high.

Compare ■ HID downlights, decorative surface luminaires, CFL downlights, CFL wall packs

CFL Downlight

Recess in canopy or soffit 8 to 12 ft high

Lamps   CFL (18, 26, and 32W)

Lamp Orientation   Vertical (base up preferred)

12" Diameter

Description ■ CFL downlights are designed to recess partially into a ceiling. Light is directed out of a round or square opening through a spread lens or dropped diffuser.

Application Tips ■ This luminaire is a good replacement for existing incandescent downlights but must have a low-temperature ballast to operate in cold weather.

Compare ■ Canopy lights, HID downlights, decorative surface luminaires, enclosed fluorescent strips

CFL Wall Pack

Surface mount 6 to 10 ft high

Lamps   CFL (23 and 28 W)

Lamp Orientation   Vertical (base up preferred)

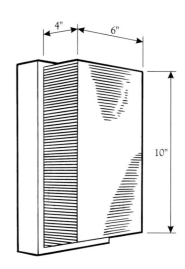

Description ■ CFL wall packs are small luminaires meant to be mounted at relatively low heights. These luminaires incorporate prismatic lenses specifically designed to direct most of the light down. Manufacturers usually offer optional vandal-resistant lenses.

Application Tips ■ This luminaire replaces existing incandescent porch or door lights and suits the same applications in new residential and commercial construction. Use luminaires with CFLs instead of HID lamps when quick starts are important.

Compare ■ Downlight wall luminaires, decorative surface luminaires

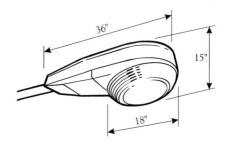

Cobrahead

Mount on an arm to a 20 to 40 ft pole

Lamps   Metal halide (175, 250, 400, and 1000 W)
                       High pressure sodium (100, 150, 250, 400, and 1000 W)
                       Mercury vapor (400 W)

Lamp Orientation   Horizontal

Description ■ The typical cobrahead has a dropped glass refractor that distributes light primarily to its sides and front. Cobraheads often appear in parking lots and as street lights.

Application Tips ■ Utilities, towns, and cities often use cobrahead luminaires as street lights, and often must grant permission for moving a cobrahead and pole. The glass refractor creates direct glare, so cutoff luminaires make good replacements in parking and area lighting installations.

Compare ■ Type III cutoffs, type V cutoffs

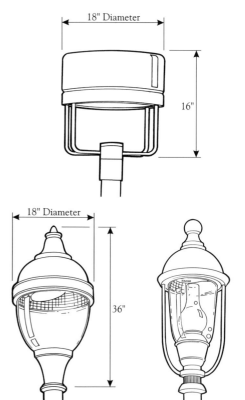

Decorative Cutoff

Mount on a pole or decorative arm 10 to 20 ft high

Lamps   Metal halide (100, 150, 175, and 250 W)
                       High pressure sodium (70, 100, and 150 W)

Lamp Orientation   Horizontal

Description ■ Decorative cutoffs offer an optics package that controls glare. Some feature a top that glows softly, while most of the light radiates downward, usually in a symmetrical circular- or square-patterned distribution. Some have a large decorative metal cap that conceals the lamp and reflector with a clear or lightly stippled globe below. This luminaire often includes a decorative chimney or a metal stem.

Application Tips ■ These luminaires incorporate the same reflector system as cutoff luminaires. The top may be a pyramid, half sphere, or cylinder that complements a contemporary architectural style. Some decorative cutoffs have a luminous top that contributes to light pollution and so may be inappropriate for some applications.

Compare ■ Performance post tops, type V cutoffs

Decorative Post Top

Mount on a pole or decorative arm 6 to 16 ft high

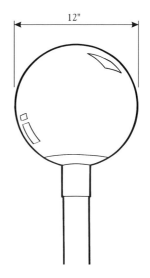

Lamps   Metal halide (50, 70, 100, and 150 W)
High pressure sodium (50, 70, and 100 W)
Dedicated compact fluorescent (28 W quad)

Lamp Orientation Vertical

Description ■ In contemporary or period styles, this luminaire serves as both light source and decoration. Primarily benefiting pedestrians, these fixtures do not distribute light efficiently. Some versions include a frosted-glass shroud that helps diffuse lamp brightness. Manufacturers usually offer standard vandal-resistant polycarbonate globes or lenses.

Application Tips ■ These fixtures typically incorporate an inexpensive, unshielded, white plastic diffusing globe, which turns yellow in sunlight and blocks almost 50 percent of the light from the lamp; much of the remaining light radiates up and away. More-efficient versions have clear plastic or frosted lenses and opaque tops or some other type of shielding to push light down and out toward the walkway and the pedestrians. UV-stabilized polycarbonate lenses resist yellowing in sunlight. The uplight contributes to light pollution.

Compare ■ Decorative cutoffs, performance post tops

Decorative Surface Luminaire

Surface mount 6 to 10 ft high

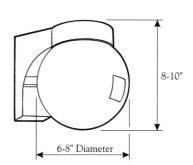

Lamps   CFL (20 and 28 W)
Screwbase CFL (18, 20, and 23 W)
Incandescent
(25 W A15) (40, 60, and 100 W A19) (150 W A21)

Lamp Orientation Vertical (base up preferred for CFL) or horizontal

Description ■ Decorative surface luminaires are meant to be mounted at relatively low heights. Decorative lanterns for CFLs, available in period and contemporary styles, replace similar incandescent luminaires. Manufacturers usually offer optional vandal-resistant globes and refractor lenses.

Application Tips ■ The CFL versions of this luminaire are good retrofits for existing incandescent porch or door lights and suit the same applications in new residential and commercial construction. Some versions are used for low soffit or canopy mounting. The use of non-screwbase CFLs prevent users from reverting to incandescent sources when replacing a burned out lamp.

Compare ■ Downlight wall luminaires, canopy lights, CFL downlights, CFL wall packs

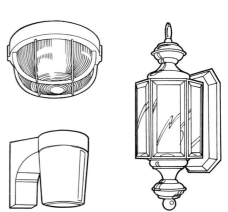

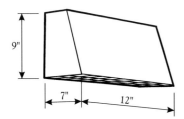

Downlight Wall Luminaire

Surface mount 9 to 15 ft high

Lamps   Metal halide (70, 100, 150, and 175 W)
High pressure sodium (70, 100, and 150 W)

Lamp Orientation   Horizontal or vertical

Description ■ Downlight wall luminaires mount directly to walls and light immediately adjacent areas. The downlight wall luminaire limits glare by concealing the lamp from the front and sides, distributing light with an internal forward- or side-throw reflector system and a diffusing lens. Vandal-resistant lenses are available.

Application Tips ■ Downlight wall luminaires function like type V cutoff luminaires and effectively light the area within two mounting heights of the wall. The downlight wall luminaire is well suited for lighting buildings where appearance is as important as security and for lighting areas frequented by elderly persons who tend to be affected more by glare.

Compare ■ Performance wall packs, shielded wall packs, CFL downlights, CFL wall packs, decorative surface luminaires.

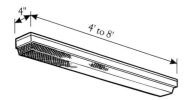

Enclosed Fluorescent Strip

Surface mount on a canopy or soffit 8 to 12 ft high

Lamps   Fluorescent 4 ft T12 (40 W)
8 ft slimline (75 W)
4 ft T8 (32 W) and 8-ft T8 (60 W)

Lamp Orientation   Horizontal

Description ■ The enclosed fluorescent strip is an all-weather version of the open fluorescent strip with an aluminum or steel housing and a high-impact-acrylic prismatic lens.

Application Tips ■ This luminaire serves as a direct replacement for open fluorescent strips and in new construction to light under canopies and soffits where limited mounting heights may eliminate the use of HID luminaires. The enclosed fluorescent strip provides an alternative to surface-mounted incandescent luminaires. Energy-saving T12 and slimline lamps should not be used in enclosed fluorescent strips because they do not start or operate reliably in temperatures below 50°F. To some extent, T8 and T12 lamp-ballast combinations use the retained warmth from the electrical arc current in these luminaires for cold-weather operation. However T8 lamps, because of their lower voltages depend even more on this source of heat. T8 lamp-ballast combinations do not start in extreme cold, even in enclosed luminaires.

Compare ■ Decorative surface luminaires, CFL downlights, CFL wall packs, canopy lights, fluorescent sign lighters, HID downlights

Flood and Sports Flood Light

Mount to a 20 to 40 ft pole or surface (higher on building tops), or grade mount

Lamps   Metal halide (150, 250, 400, and 1000 W)
                     High pressure sodium (100, 150, 250, 400, and 1000 W)

Lamp Orientation Vertical or horizontal

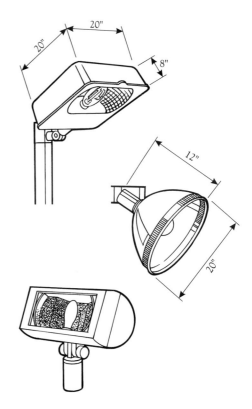

Description ■ Flood lights blanket an area with light; however, their internal optics control the exact pattern of light distribution, which ranges from tight circles to large squares and rectangles. Flood lights are usually rectangular, but the rounded sports flood light is particularly effective from high above the ground, distributing light in a circular pattern. Manufacturers of flood lights and sports flood lights offer optional, vandal-resistant shields.

Application Tips ■ Flood lights should be carefully located and aimed to optimize coverage, control glare, and minimize light trespass. Flood lights on poles, often used to light lots or yards, should not be aimed more than 60 degrees above vertical, and should normally be mounted no lower than 20-ft high. Grade- or ground-mounted floodlights for uplighting building facades should not be mounted more than three-quarters of a building's height from the building, or more than twice the setback apart.

Compare ■ Type III cutoffs, type V cutoffs, performance wall packs, fluorescent sign lighters

Fluorescent Sign Lighter

Mount on a 2 to 4 ft arm above or below a vertical surface

Lamps   Fluorescent 4 ft T12 (40 W)
                     8 ft slimline (75 W)
                     4 ft T8 (32 W) and 8-ft T8 (60W)

Lamp Orientation Horizontal

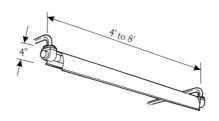

Description ■ The luminaire includes a rounded metal housing designed to distribute light across the face of a sign or building. Ballasts are often remotely mounted. Manufacturers usually offer optional impact-resistant lenses.

Application Tips ■ The fluorescent sign lighter can effectively wash a building facade with light from either below or above. Enclosed versions are a good idea when lighting from below because they clean more easily than unenclosed versions and prevent birds from nesting. However, the lenses also gather dirt and need to be cleaned regularly for optimum light output. T8 lamp-ballast combinations do not start in extreme cold, even in enclosed luminaires.

Compare ■ Flood lights, downlight wall luminaires, type III cutoffs

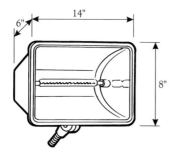

Halogen Flood Light

Surface mount

Lamps   Tubular halogen T3 (300, 350, 500, 900, and 1000 W)

Lamp Orientation   Horizontal

Description ■ The halogen flood light is a simple fixture that has an aluminum housing and heat-tempered glass lens. The scoop-shaped housing, which is polished on the inside, serves as the reflector for the slender halogen lamp. Manufacturers usually offer optional, metal lens guards.

Application Tips ■ Flood lights using halogen lamps are much less expensive to purchase than those using HID lamps; however, lamps for HID luminaires have greater light output and efficacy and longer average rated lamp life than halogen lamps, adding to the performance advantages of HID luminaires.

Compare ■ Flood lights, performance wall packs, shielded wall packs, downlight wall luminaires, type III cutoffs, CFL wall packs

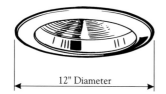

HID Downlight

Recess in a canopy or soffit
    10 to 12 ft high (50 and 70 W HID lamps)
    15 to 17 ft high (100 W HPS lamps and 100 and 150 W metal halide lamps)
    20 ft high (150 W HPS and 175 and 250 W metal halide lamps)

Lamps   Metal halide (50, 70, 100, 150, 175, and 250 W)
                            High pressure sodium (50, 70, 100, and 150 W)

Lamp Orientation   Vertical or horizontal

Description ■ A fresnel spread-lens or dropped diffuser gives this luminaire the ability to direct light to vertical as well as horizontal surfaces.

Application Tips ■ The fully recessed version is a good choice where a clean ceiling line is desirable. HID downlights usually recess at least 10 inches into the ceiling and may not be suitable as retrofits where ceilings are shallow. Open luminaires are available that must be used with HPS lamps or metal halide lamps suitable for use in open luminaires.

Compare ■ Canopy lights, decorative surface luminaires, CFL downlights, CFL wall packs, fluorescent sign lighters

Incandescent Downlight

Recess in a soffit 8 to 15 ft high

Lamps   Incandescent (A19 100 W) and (A21 150 W)

Lamp Orientation   Vertical or horizontal

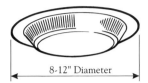

8-12" Diameter

Description ■ The recessed incandescent downlight includes a dropped or prismatic-glass lens and has at least a 6-inch recessed depth.

Application Tips ■ Recessed CFL and low-wattage HID downlights can often be installed as replacement luminaires for incandescent downlights using existing locations and wiring. Open luminaires are also available.

Compare ■ Canopy lights, open fluorescent strips, decorative surface luminaires, CFL downlights, CFL wall packs, HID downlights

Open Fluorescent Strip

Surface mount on a canopy or soffit 8 to 12 ft high

Lamps   Fluorescent 4 ft T12 (40 W)
                        8 ft slimline (75 W)

Lamp Orientation   Horizontal

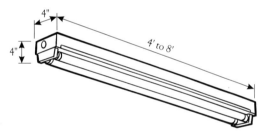

Description ■ A metal channel encloses the ballast and serves as a mount for a single lamp or two parallel lamps.

Application Tips ■ Fluorescent lamps with high CRIs replace older fluorescent lamps, some of which have been eliminated by national energy legislation. Energy-saving T12 and slimline lamps and T8 lamps, except for high-output versions, should not be used in open fluorescent strips because they do not start or operate reliably in temperatures below 50°F, even when using the most modern ballast technology. Lamps used in open strips need to be cleaned regularly.

Compare ■ Decorative surface luminaires, CFL downlights, CFL wall packs, canopy lights

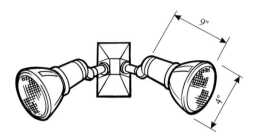

PAR Lamp Holder

Surface mount

Lamps

PAR38 (150W)
Halogen PAR38 (90, 120, and 150 W)
Halogen IR PAR38 (60 and 100 W)

Lamp Orientation   Variable

Description ■ Homeowners often mount these medium-base lamp holders on junction boxes to light the perimeters of their homes and driveways or alleys.

Application Tips ■ Replacements for the PAR lamp holder include much higher-efficacy HID or compact fluorescent lamps in low-glare wall packs or other appropriate low-glare luminaires. PAR lamp holders can easily accommodate a motion sensor; however, they can also become sources of direct glare.

Compare ■ Performance wall packs, shielded wall packs, downlight wall luminaires, type III cutoffs, CFL wall packs

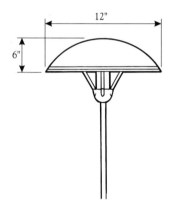

Path Light

Grade mount on a 15 to 18-inch-high stem

Lamps   A-lamp (25 and 40 W)

Lamp Orientation   Vertical

Description ■ Common styles of path lights feature either a metal hat, which shields the lamp from view and directs light down and out, or a cylindrical opal lens with metal louvers and top. Both mount atop metal stems, which are usually ½-inch diameter metal rods of the same finish as the luminaires. These luminaires light an area about 4-5 ft in diameter.

Application Tips ■ Path lights less expensive than bollards and less durable. Path lights are not suited for applications where vandalism is likely.

Compare ■ Bollards, performance post tops

Pendant Uplight

Suspend from a ceiling

Lamps   Metal halide (175, 250, and 400 W)
                     High pressure sodium (150, 250, and 400 W)

Lamp Orientation   Horizontal

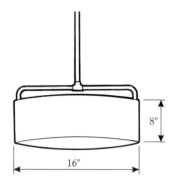

Description ■ The pendant uplight comprises an opaque enclosure with an open or lensed top that directs light upward. The lensed-top version is more suitable for outdoor use, but it requires periodic cleaning.

Application Tips ■ Gazebos and porte cocheres often have high or vaulted ceilings and can benefit from indirect lighting from this luminaire. In most cases, 36 inches must be allowed from the ceiling to allow the uplight to spread.

Compare ■ Canopy lights, HID downlights

Performance Post Top

Mount on a pole or decorative arm 10 to 20 ft high

Lamps   Metal halide (70, 100, 150, and 250 W)
                     High pressure sodium (70, 100, and 150 W)
                     CFL (26 and 32 W)

Lamp Orientation   Vertical or horizontal

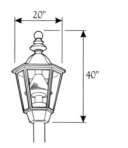

Description ■ The performance post top's distinctive feature is its housing, which is typically a period lantern or transparent globe. Performance post tops distribute light and control glare more effectively than unshielded white plastic globes that block almost 50 percent of the light from the lamp. A prismatic lens or refractive lamp shroud may redirect light down and out to the walkway or street. Some performance post tops feature a multiple-reflector device around the lamp for the same purpose. Manufacturers usually offer standard vandal-resistant globes and lamps.

Application Tips ■ Pole- and building-mounted versions add flexibility for lighting a complicated area. Also, clustering several luminaires on one pole adds emphasis to a special location such as an intersection or building entry.

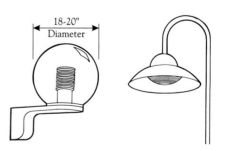

Compare ■ Decorative cutoffs, type III cutoffs, type V cutoffs

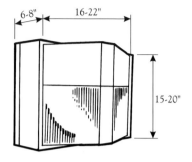

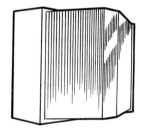

Performance Wall Pack

Surface mount 12 to 20 ft high

Lamps   Metal halide (100, 150, and 175 W)
High pressure sodium (70, 100, and 150 W)

Lamp Orientation   Horizontal or vertical

Description ■ Primarily for security lighting of building perimeters, these luminaires include precisely-designed internal reflectors and specially engineered refractors that control glare. Manufacturers usually offer standard vandal-resistant lenses.

Application Tips ■ Light distributions vary depending on internal optics. Side-throw versions provide broad, shallow distributions meant to maximize spacing distances. Forward-throw versions distribute light far into the site with a low cutoff angle.

Compare ■ Shielded wall packs, downlight wall luminaires, type III cutoffs, CFL wall packs

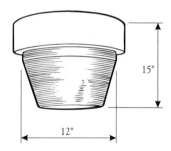

Refractor Basket

Surface mount 8 to 10 ft high (parking garages)

Lamps   Metal halide (100 and 175 W)
High pressure sodium (100 and 150 W)

Lamp Orientation   Vertical

Description ■ The distinguishing characteristic of the refractor basket is its blunt-nosed, cone-shaped prismatic lens. The lens mounts to a metal housing.

Application Tips ■ At the low mounting heights typical of parking garages, glare from the refractor basket can be significant. Light may be distributed only within a very small circle, leaving the walls largely unlighted.

Compare ■ Enclosed fluorescent strips, shielded garage luminaires

Shielded Garage Luminaire

Surface or pendant mount

Lamps   Metal halide (100 and 175 W)
                       High pressure sodium (100 and 150 W)

Lamp Orientation   Vertical

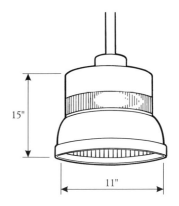

Description ▪ The garage luminaire is specifically designed for parking garages, providing both up and downlighting. Uplighting is achieved through a window of clear polycarbonate in the housing. The lamp is shielded from direct view from the side by either an opaque or prismatic section. An internal reflector system distributes downlighting through a clear polycarbonate lens on the bottom of the luminaire.

Application Tips ▪ The uplight component of the garage luminaire helps illuminate the ceiling of the parking garage, reducing the difference in brightness between the light source and the dark ceiling and reducing glare. These luminaires generally provide a type V circular or square distribution of downlight.

Compare ▪ Enclosed fluorescent strip

Shielded Wall Pack

Surface mount 9 to 15 ft high

Lamps   Metal halide (70, 100, 150, and 175 W)
                       High pressure sodium (70, 100, and 150 W)

Lamp Orientation   Horizontal or vertical

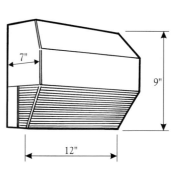

Description ▪ Wall packs mount directly to walls and light immediately adjacent areas. Shielded wall packs employ either opaque panels or diffusing lenses to block direct views of the lamp from the front or sides. Manufacturers usually offer vandal-resistant lenses as a standard feature.

Application Tips ▪ Shielded wall packs light the area within approximately two mounting heights of the wall.

Compare ▪ Downlight wall luminaires, performance wall packs, decorative surface luminaires, CFL wall packs

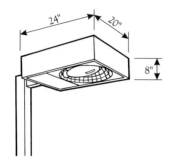

Type III Cutoff

Mount on a bracket arm to a pole or surface 15 to 40 ft high

Lamps   Metal halide (100, 150, 250, 400, and 1000 W)
                      High pressure sodium (100, 150, 250, and 400 W)

Lamp Orientation Horizontal

Description ■ Also called a shoe box or sharp cutoff, this luminaire effectively lights parking lots, walkways, and streets. It controls glare at angles below horizontal and distributes light mostly to its front and sides, with some light behind, in a pattern called type III distribution. Manufacturers offer impact-resistant shields.

Application Tips ■ For best uniformity, leave about four times the mounting height between poles. Two fixtures mounted back to back on the same pole provide a rectangular light distribution around the pole that covers more area than a single unit. An optional internal house-side shield eliminates most of the light from the rear of the fixture.

Compare ■ Type V cutoffs, decorative cutoffs, performance post tops, fluorescent sign lighters

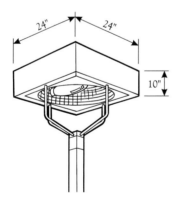

Type V Cutoff

Yoke mount on pole, bracket arm, or ceiling 25 to 50 ft high

Lamps   Metal halide (250, 400, and 1000 W)
                      High pressure sodium (250, 400, and 1000 W)

Lamp Orientation Horizontal or vertical

Description ■ The type V cutoff luminaire controls glare at angles below horizontal and distributes light symmetrically around a pole in either a circular or square pattern called type V distribution. Manufacturers usually offer optional impact-resistant shields.

Application Tips ■ Often associated with high-wattage lamps and tall poles, this luminaire effectively lights large areas such as parking lots adjacent to shopping centers. For good uniformity, space poles up to five times the pole height.

Compare ■ Type III cutoffs, decorative cutoffs, performance post tops

Wall Pack

Surface mount 12 to 20 ft high

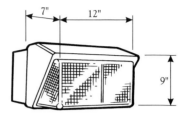

Lamps	Metal halide (100, 150, and 175 W)
	High pressure sodium (70, 100, and 150 W)
Lamp Orientation	Horizontal

Description ■ The wall pack provides lighting for building perimeters. It is usually shielded at the top but does little to control glare. Wall pack manufacturers offer optional vandal-resistant polycarbonate refractors.

Application Tips ■ Shielded and performance wall packs and directional wall luminaires control glare better than standard wall packs.

Compare ■ Shielded wall packs, decorative surface luminaires, performance wall packs, downlight wall luminaires, CFL wall packs

Yard Light

Mount on a bracket arm to a pole or surface

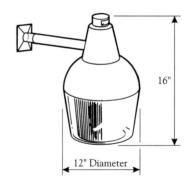

Lamps	Mercury vapor (100 and 175 W)
Lamp Orientation	Vertical

Description ■ The bluish-white light of the mercury vapor yard light has been a security and street lighting staple for many years. Its cylindrical prismatic refractor, often open at the bottom, produces direct glare and casts a small circle of light on the ground. An optional refractor adds vandal resistance.

Application Tips ■ HPS and metal halide lamps in more-efficient, glare-control luminaires provide more light output per watt and better light distribution than the mercury vapor yard light. Although some newer yard lights house HPS and metal halide lamps, the luminaire's inherent glare and inefficiency reduce the benefits to be gained by using these lamps.

Compare ■ Type III cutoffs, type V cutoffs, decorative cutoffs, performance post tops

CONTROLS

The lighting controls available for luminaires used in outdoor lighting include the simple switch, which provides manual on-off control. Interval timers, motion detectors, photosensors, and time clocks provide automatic switching, dimming at preset times, or minimum light levels when people enter a space. Even HID lamps can be dimmed, using two-level dimming technology.

Interval timer

Description An interval timer allows lights to be switched on manually, and turns them off automatically after a preset time has elapsed. An interval timer usually comprises a push-button switch located on a light pole, a timer with a variable time limit (usually 10 minutes to several hours), and an electrical contactor or relay system that connects the lights in the area to the control system. The timer and contactor or relay system are usually near the circuit breaker panel.

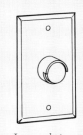

Interval timer pushbutton remote

Table of Contents

Application Tips Where lighting is needed for short times, such as tennis courts, interval timers often replace standard switches. Where lighting is needed only for certain short-term tasks or for a sense of security during temporary use, interval timers are an alternative to motion detectors. However, people passing through or using an area may need light longer than the preset time and be forced to go back to the timer to reset it. Timers can control lamps in one or more luminaires and can be wall- or pole-mounted at standard switch height.

Motion Detector

Description Motion detectors, often called occupancy sensors, automatically switch on incandescent and fluorescent lamps upon detecting motion. Only infrared sensors, which respond to the motion of an infrared-heat source, should be used for outdoor applications.

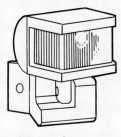

Motion detector

Ultrasonic sensors can detect motion as slight as air movement, and so are generally too sensitive for outdoor use. A motion detector-photosensor combination switches lights only at night.

Application Tips Motion detectors can save energy and can extend the service life of lamps by turning lamps off when an area is unoccupied. Although frequent switching of fluorescent lamps reduces the number of hours the lamps operate, service life may increase because the lamps are off for periods of time when they might have been operating. Motion detectors are not suitable controls for HID lamps because these lamps require up to several minutes to start-up and to restrike. A motion detector mounted on a building face or luminaire pole can control several luminaires, but the motion detector must be positioned to sense movement at the entry of the area to be lighted. Some luminaires include motion detectors that mount directly on their housings, controlling only lamps within the luminaire. The performance of motion detectors varies; manufacturers provide information describing the proper use of their products.

Photosensor

Description   A photosensor switches a luminaire on when the surrounding light level drops below a specified level. Photosensors typically operate outdoor luminaires from dusk to dawn, but can also turn lights on during a period of reduced light during the day.

Application Tips   A luminaire may include an integral photosensor mounted directly to the luminaire's housing. Several luminaires can be controlled by a central photosensor, usually building mounted and facing north to eliminate the effects of direct sunlight at dawn or dusk. Photosensors can also operate together with a motion detector or with a time clock to turn lights on at dusk and off at a pre-selected time.

Switch

Description   Switches are manual controls that turn lamps on and off. These controls are usually located on a wall at an entrance. The most common, a single-pole switch, operates one or more luminaires from a single location.

Application Tips   Manual switches can save energy only if people turn lamps off when leaving an area or light is not needed. People will be more likely to use a switch if it is in a convenient location.

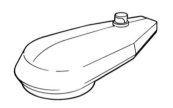

Integral photosensor with cobrahead

Time Clock

Description   Time clocks can be used to switch lamps according to a programmed schedule. They may be electro-mechanical or electronic. Some electronic versions can be programmed for a seven-day week or even a school year complete with holidays; other time clocks allow only a single daily schedule.

Application Tips   The most common application of a time clock is in conjunction with a central photosensor. Often, the photosensor turns the lamps on at dusk and the time clock turns them off at some predetermined time. Time clocks are sometimes used to turn lamps both on and off at times that correspond to dusk and dawn; these devices sometimes include an astronomic dial that corrects for seasonal changes of sunrise and sunset.

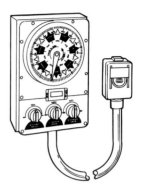

Photosensor and time clock

Two-Level Dimming Ballasts for HID Lamps

Description   Two-level, or bi-level, dimming ballasts allow HID lamps to be dimmed from full light output to a reduced level in one step. The use of two-level dimming results in a fixed power and light output reduction. The exact power use at reduced settings and minimum light output setting vary by manufacturer, but can be as little as 30-40 percent of maximum power and 10-20 percent of maximum light output.

Application Tips   Parking lot owners sometimes switch several luminaires off after normal working hours in an effort to save energy, but this strategy can result in areas of darkness. As an alternative, a two-level dimming system activated by a time clock could lower the light output of all the HID luminaires at a preset time, resulting in lower energy use and a reduced, but uniform, light level.

Appendix

Ballasts

Ballasts are components of HID and fluorescent lighting systems and can affect the performance of the system and the life of the lamps. HID and fluorescent lamp ballasts, which are available in magnetic and electronic versions, provide proper starting voltage and regulated operating current to lamps. Ballasts add to the power (in watts) required to operate a lighting system: the rated power of the lamps in a system is usually less than the input power of the system.

Good sources of information about ballast performance include manufacturers' literature and the National Lighting Product Information Program at Rensselaer Polytechnic Institute's Lighting Research Center (LRC), which supplies useful manufacturer-specific information about ballast types and performance. In addition the American National Standards Institute (ANSI) has developed specifications for ballast performance.

Ballast service life may be 20 years or longer so many older ballasts remain in operation today. Maintenance personnel should be aware that older ballasts sometimes leak fluids that may contain polychlorinated biphenyls (PCBs), which is a hazardous material.

The label "No PCBs" appears on ballasts manufactured after 1978. The U.S. Environmental Protection Agency maintains 12 regional offices that offer information about finding state regulations for handling and disposal of all PCB-laden ballasts.

Fluorescent Lamp Ballasts

Most fluorescent lamp ballasts include a preheat, rapid-start, or instant-start circuit. In most cases the specifier or the contractor will determine which is the appropriate circuit for an outdoor lighting application. The starting curcuit of a lamp must be compatible with the starting circuit of its ballasts or the lamp may perform poorly, fail to start, or burn out prematurely. The LRC and manufacturers provide literature that explains lamp-ballast compatibility.

The starting circuit of a preheat ballast heats a lamp's electrodes for several seconds before initiating current flow and striking the lamp's arc. These simple and inexpensive ballasts provide reliable starting in cold environments; however, the compact fluorescent lamps and short, linear fluorescent lamps that often operate using preheat ballasts may flash when starting.

Rapid-start ballasts, which commonly operate 4-ft T12 and T8 lamps, apply 3-4 volts (V) to heat the lamp's electrodes and then apply approximately 200-300 V to the lamp, which starts after a second or two without flashing. Lamps operating on rapid-start ballasts do not start reliably at temperatures lower than 50°F, although low-temperature versions of the ballast are available. Rapid-start ballasts, except cathode-disconnect versions, also require 3-4 watts to heat the electrodes during operation, slightly increasing the cost of operating rapid-start systems.

Instant-start ballasts apply 400-1000 V directly to the lamp's electrodes, which starts a lamp with no delay and no preheating. The high starting voltage may damage a lamp's electrodes, which can reduce lamp life by as much as 25 percent from its rated value if the lamps operate less than an average of 6 hours per start. Instant-start ballasts are most often used to start and operate slimline lamps, which have heavy-duty electrodes that better withstand the high lamp starting voltages.

Magnetic fluorescent lamp ballasts usually operate lamps at 60 Hz. They are filled with a heavy potting compound that reduces noise and dissipates heat. Since 1990, United States federal law has prohibited the manufacture and sale of the low-efficiency magnetic ballasts that were standard for many years; the law allows only energy-efficient models with higher-quality components to be used in commercial applications.

Hybrid ballasts, also known as cathode-disconnect ballasts, are basically rapid-start magnetic ballasts with electronic circuits that discontinue electrode-heating after the lamp starts, saving about 3 or 4 W during operation.

Electronic ballasts typically operate lamps at frequencies of 20,000 kHz or higher. The high-frequency operation of the fluorescent lamps eliminates the often-perceptible flicker associated with 60-Hz low-frequency operation and increases lamp efficacy by about 10 percent. Instant-start electronic ballasts also start and run lamps without providing additional wattage to heat the lamp electrodes.

HID Lamp Ballasts

Luminaire manufacturers help determine the appropriate ballasts for the specifier's lamp and luminaire selection. Each HID lamp type (metal halide, high pressure sodium, and mercury vapor) and wattage has unique starting and operating requirements that require a ballast to be specific to lamp type and wattage. For instance, a HPS ballast will not operate a metal halide or mercury vapor lamp and a 400-W HID lamp ballast will not operate a 250-W HID lamp, no matter the lamp.

Although HID ballasts are available in magnetic and electronic versions, the magnetic versions are more widely available for the high-wattage lamps used in large-area, outdoor lighting applications.

Input voltage varies from one application to another. For instance, service to residential applications is usually 120 or 240 V, while service at commercial facilities might be 120, 208, 240, 277, or 480 V. Luminaire manufacturers match input voltages with ballast circuits (e.g., reactor, constant-wattage, constant wattage autotransformer, and autotransformer reactor). Some ballasts can operate on only one input voltage while others, called multi-tap ballasts, can accept one of several input voltages.

HID lamps are used in a variety of luminaire housings, requiring a number of different ballast configurations. The most common, and least expensive, configuration is the core-and-coil, which consists of a laminated steel core, a copper coil, and other circuitry, all usually mounted on a metal plate, which itself mounts to the inside of a luminaire housing. Core-and-coil ballasts may be placed in a potting resin, to reduce noise from the ballast.

All potted core-and-coil ballasts are enclosed in a metal box. Some HID lamp ballasts must be mounted remotely because the luminaire is too small to allow internal mounting. Post-mounted luminaires require a weatherproof core-and-coil ballast, which fits in a slender weatherproof box that can be mounted inside a pole. These ballasts can also be remotely mounted when the luminaire is surface mounted.

Lighting Equipment Materials

The quality of materials used for the housings, reflectors, lenses, and gaskets of luminaires vary greatly and affect the price and performance of the luminaires. Poles, too, vary in quality of material, price, and durability.

Housings

Housings are the external shells of luminaires, enclosing the lamp, the reflector, and for fluorescent and HID lamps, usually the ballast. A housing must protect these components from the environment outside the luminaire, which would otherwise damage the components, ruining the performance of the luminaire and causing premature failure. The housings of outdoor luminaires are usually manufactured of steel, aluminum, or plastic.

Steel housings provide better structural strength and cost less than other metals. Sheet steel housings are the most common and inexpensive steel housings; the housings of economically priced flood lights, wall packs, downlights, quartz flood lights, cutoff luminaires, and open fluorescent strips are often steel sheet.

Steel sheet must be coated or finished, or it will rust and corrode. Steel sheet may be galvanized, which is a finishing process that deposits zinc electrochemically on the steel, providing a silver-colored coat that withstands normal outdoor environments well but may corrode in salt-air and harsh chemical environments.

Steel sheet can be painted, usually with a factory-applied, baked-on coating of enamel or electrostatically-applied polyester powder that is available in a wide variety of colors. Paint processes have improved in recent years and generally provide reliable protection against the outdoor environment. However, a scratch can leave the steel vulnerable to corrosion and rust.

Housings of stainless steel, a steel alloy containing chromium, resist corrosion and are very expensive. Luminaires installed in salt air or other highly corrosive environments often have stainless steel housings. Downlights, canopy lights, and decorative surface luminaires may have stainless steel housings, but more often only some components, such as hinges, springs, latches, and fasteners are stainless steel.

Housings of aluminum and aluminum alloys can also survive in salt air and other corrosive outdoor environments, and these housings are less expensive than stainless steel housings. Aluminum housings can be extruded, cast, fabricated from a sheet, or spun.

Extruded aluminum housings are formed by forcing semi-soft aluminum through a die of the shape of the housing to produce a continuously formed piece; extruded aluminum housings are generally more expensive than other aluminum housings. Extrusions are commonly used for cutoff luminaires, canopy lights, bollards, downlight wall luminaires, and fluorescent sign lighters.

Housings with rounded edges or some other feature that does not lend itself to extruding are usually manufactured of cast, or die-cast, aluminum. Manufacturers make cast-aluminum housings by pouring molten aluminum alloy into a two-piece mold, or die, and splitting the mold open once the metal cools. Because cast-aluminum housings are often one-piece, they are less likely to leak than housings with welded joints. Examples of cast-housing luminaires are canopy lights, wall packs, cobraheads, decorative surface and cutoff luminaires, flood lights, PAR lamp holders, performance post tops, and lensed cutoffs.

Fabricated aluminum sheet is like sheet steel, except with the corrosion-resistance of aluminum. Manufacturers often use sheet aluminum to form the top of an extruded aluminum cutoff luminaire.

Spun aluminum, which is made by conforming an aluminum sheet to the shape of a chuck on a spinning lathe, is usually reserved for the simple, rounded housing shapes used in some sports flood lights. Spun aluminum housings are often thinner and generally less sturdy and durable than other aluminum housings.

Aluminum housings can be painted like steel or anodized. The smooth surface of extruded aluminum is often anodized. The metal is dipped in a chemical bath that causes the formation of a thick exterior layer of aluminum oxide. This protective barrier, usually warranteed by the manufacturer, does not scratch as easily as paint; however, anodized aluminum is available in only a few colors. Organic dyes added to the chemical bath allows for more colors (dye anodizing). Sunlight fades dye-anodized finishes more quickly than standard anodized finishes. Cast aluminum housings are too porous to be anodized and are usually painted.

Thermoplastics like acrylic and polycarbonate are also used as materials for luminaire housings. Formed by the application of heat and pressure, thermoplastic housings retain their shapes under normal conditions, are lighter than metal housings, and since they resist corrosion without special coatings, are less expensive to manufacture than metal housings. Standard acrylics, however, tend to be breakable. Manufacturers have developed high-impact versions that resist vandalism. Ultraviolet (UV) exposure does not significantly affect acrylic housings; but these housings yellow only after many years.

UV-stabilized polycarbonates, by contrast, are very durable and are often used for vandal-resistant housings. Non-UV-stabilized polycarbonates degrade, becoming discolored and brittle, under exposure to UV from the sun. Both acrylics and polycarbonates are vulnerable to heat and are not usually used with incandescent lamps.

Reflectors

In most outdoor luminaires, a reflector distributes light by redirecting it from the lamp. The materials and construction of the reflector system largely determine how well a luminaire performs, and to some degree, how much it costs. Virtually all reflectors used in outdoor luminaires are made of hydroformed, spun, or segmented aluminum.

Hydroformed aluminum reflectors are the most common in outdoor applications; they are economical to manufacture in large quantities and perform consistently. Spun aluminum reflectors are the least expensive to produce, but they are usually thinner and less durable than hydroformed versions.

Some outdoor luminaires incorporate a segmented reflector system, fabricated from specially designed aluminum strips that are bent at angles to provide precise light distributions. Many specifiers believe that segmented reflectors provide the best performance, but luminaires with segmented reflectors usually cost more than than those with other reflector types.

Aluminum reflectors are polished or chemically brightened to enhance their ability to reflect light. Reflective, or specular, reflectors generally add more to the cost of the luminaire than do semi-specular reflectors.

Lenses and shields

Although a housing provides a great deal of protection for the lamp and reflector, most luminaires have a glass or plastic lens or shield that covers the opening through which light exits the luminaire. A shield is usually clear and simply allows light to pass through while a lens redirects the light and scatters the lamp image. Glass shields and lenses are generally heat-tempered versions of either soda-lime glass or borosilicate glass. Heat tempering helps the glass resist the high temperatures near a light source and also adds some measure of impact resistance. Soda-lime glass is the standard glass used for windows and is inexpensive to form. Borosilicate glass is more expensive to fabricate, but resists much higher temperatures than soda glass.

The most common plastics used for lenses and shields are clear, white, or tinted acrylics and polycarbonates, which are lighter than glass. Acrylics are not as fragile as glass and retain color (white and tinted versions) or clarity (clear versions) well even when subjected to heat from lamps and to ultraviolet light. Polycarbonates are much tougher than acrylics and are often used as vandal-resistant lenses or shields. Polycarbonates withstand heat even better than acrylics do, but will yellow and turn cloudy with exposure to UV.

Gaskets

Gaskets are seals between components of an outdoor luminaire to seal out dirt, bugs, and corrosive air-borne chemicals. A poor gasketing system allows debris and chemicals to enter the luminaire, which corrodes the reflector, and settle on the lens, impeding the luminaire's ability to distribute light.

Gaskets must be continuous and permanently attached to one surface so as to not loosen or fall off during luminaire maintenance. Commonly used gasketing materials include felt, sponge neoprene, and high-compliance silicone. Foam-rubber gaskets are not as durable as these other materials but are still used in some inexpensive luminaires. Felt and neoprene materials can deform, creating gaps that admit water, insects, and dirt. Silicone gaskets usually maintain their effectiveness because silicone does not permanently deform over time; however, these gaskets add more to the cost of luminaires.

Poles

Poles for outdoor luminaires are generally made from steel or aluminum. Steel is the most common pole material because of its excellent structural strength and because steel poles are less expensive to produce than aluminum poles are. Like steel housings, steel poles require a finish, usually paint or galvanization, as protection from the environment.

Aluminum poles are often preferred for aesthetic reasons, but because aluminum is not as strong as steel, an aluminum pole must be larger in cross-section or have a thicker wall than a steel pole of similar height and structural strength. The additional aluminum is the primary reason that aluminum poles are more expensive than steel poles. Like aluminum housings, aluminum poles can be painted or anodized.

Decorative poles reminiscent of those from the early days of outdoor lighting are offered in a variety of materials. The original poles were cast iron, and while this material is still available, most manufacturers of decorative poles use cast aluminum, a much lighter and less expensive material. Fiberglass, which can be cast into molds, is even less expensive than cast aluminum but less durable.

Glossary

A-lamp: the common incandescent light bulb used in most homes in North America. An A-lamp can have a clear, white-coated, or etched-frost glass envelope.

Acrylic: a plastic used to shield the lamps in luminaires or to distribute the luminous intensity, or both. Acrylic resists yellowing from ultraviolet radiation, but becomes brittle.

Adaptation: the process by which the human visual system adjusts to light levels. Complete adaptation takes considerable time, especially when changing from a light to a dark environment.

Aiming: the process of directing the light distribution from a luminaire toward the object or area to be lighted. Proper aiming is critical to prevent direct glare.

Annual operating cost: the cost per year of electricity and maintenance of a lighting system, including replacement parts and associated labor.

Anodizing: a process for chemically treating aluminum to provide a durable, protective finish.

ANSI: American National Standards Institute. ANSI coordinates and approves the processes for developing voluntary national standards, including those related to the lighting industry.

Arc: an electrical discharge through an ionized gaseous atmosphere. Fluorescent and HID lamps are examples of light sources that use an arc to produce light.

Arc tube: an envelope, usually quartz or ceramic, that contains the arc of a discharge light source.

Area of calculation: a lighted surface over which numerical values (illuminance or luminance) are calculated. Values may be given for particular points within the area of calculation, or may be an average of all points within the area.

Area lighting: lighting provided to illuminate open areas uniformly.

ASHRAE: American Society of Heating, Refrigerating, and Air-Conditioning Engineers. ASHRAE, in conjunction with IESNA, has developed standards for energy efficiency in new and existing buildings. Lighting, including exterior lighting, is an important part of the ASHRAE/IES Standard 90.1, *Energy Efficient Design of New Buildings Except Low-Rise Residential Buildings*.

Astronomic timer: a control that changes its settings based upon seasonal daylight variations.

Average rated lamp life: the time in hours for a given percent (often 50 percent) of a large group of lamps to fail under standardized operating conditions. For fluorescent lamps, the conditions include cycles of operation at nominal line voltage at 3 hours per start. For HID lamps, the lamps are operated at 10 hours per start. Any individual lamp, or group of lamps, may vary from the published average rated life.

Average to minimum (avg:min): the ratio of average numerical value (illuminance or luminance) to the minimum value found within a lighted area. It is one of the measures used to indicate lighting uniformity.

Ballast: a device that provides the necessary voltage, current, and wave form for starting and operating fluorescent or HID lamps.

Beam spread: the width, expressed in degrees, of a light beam from a reflector lamp. The edge of the beam is typically defined as the point at which the luminous intensity is 50 percent as great as at the center of the beam. See also center beam candlepower (CBCP).

Bollard: a low post-shaped luminaire, typically 3 to 4 ft in height, used to light pathways, walkways, and perimeters.

Brightness: the subjective impression of the amount of light reaching the eye. Brightness correlates approximately with luminance, a photometric measurement.

Bulb: the outer glass envelope of a light source.

Candlepower: see luminous intensity.

Center beam candlepower (CBCP): the luminous intensity (in candelas) of a reflector lamp, measured at the center of the beam.

Color rendering index (CRI): a measure of the color shift objects undergo when illuminated by a light source relative to incandescent or daylight of the same CCT.

Color temperature: see correlated color temperature.

Compact fluorescent lamp: a fluorescent lamp with a tube diameter of $5/8$ inch or less (T5) having one or more bends in the tube(s).

Constant wattage (CW) ballast: a magnetic ballast used for mercury vapor and high pressure sodium lamps, providing the best lamp-wattage regulation available. The CW ballast provides constant wattage for changes in line voltage of ±10 percent.

Constant wattage autotransformer (CWA) ballast: a magnetic ballast for HID lamps that uses a transformer in conjunction with a reactor (a coil wound on an iron core), as well as a capacitor in series with the lamp, to provide stability when voltage fluctuates ±10 percent.

Contrast: the luminance of an object related to its immediate background. See also luminance contrast.

Control: a device or system that turns lamps on and off, or dims them. Controls include switches, dimmers, timing devices, motion detectors, photosensors, and central control systems.

Correlated color temperature (CCT): an indication of the color appearance of a light source, measured in kelvin (K). The CCT rating of a lamp is a general measure of its warmth or coolness. Lamps with a CCT rating below 3500 K are generally considered warm sources, while lamps above 3500 K are considered cool sources.

Current: a rate of flow of electricity, measured in amperes (A).

Cutoff luminaire: an outdoor luminaire having light distribution characteristics designed to reduce luminous intensity at angles above 65° from vertical. Cutoff luminaires generally provide well-defined patterns of light.

Diffuser: a device that redirects or scatters light from a source.

Dimmer: a device used to vary the luminous intensity of light from a lamp. Dimmers may be electronic or magnetic, and can dim smoothly or in discrete steps.

Direct glare: excessive brightness from a source of light in the line of sight. Luminaires with poor optical control can be sources of direct glare.

Distribution: see light distribution.

Efficacy (of a light source): the total light output of a light source divided by the total input power. Efficacy is expressed in lumens per watt.

Efficiency (of a luminaire): the ratio of luminous flux (lumens) of a luminaire to the luminous flux of the lamp(s) alone. Luminous efficiency is a dimensionless measure, expressing the percentage of initial lamp lumens that exit the luminaire.

Electrode: the structure that serves as electric terminals at each end of electric discharge lamps. The electrodes of fluorescent lamps are made of coiled tungsten, covered with an emissive paste. Electrodes in HID lamps are heavier post-like structures capable of carrying high current.

Electronic ballast: a ballast that uses electronic circuitry, rather than magnetic components, to provide the voltage, current, and waveform to start and operate lamps. Electronic ballasts typically operate lamps at very high frequencies.

Energy: the product of power (watts) and time (hours). Energy used for lighting can be saved by reducing the power required or the time lighting is used, or both.

EPACT: the United States Energy Policy Act of 1992. This legislation mandated efficacy and color requirements that caused the elimination of many incandescent R and PAR lamps and full-wattage, low-CRI fluorescent lamps, among other energy-saving measures.

Facade: exterior vertical surface of a building.

Filament: a fine wire that is electrically heated to incandescence.

Fitting: (chiefly British) see luminaire.

Fixture: see luminaire.

Flood lamp: a reflector lamp that produces a wide beam of light.

Flood light: a luminaire that produces a relatively wide beam of light.

Fluorescence: the ability of some materials, such as phosphors, to convert ultraviolet energy into visible light.

Fluorescent lamp: a lamp containing mercury under low pressure, relative to high intensity discharge lamps. The mercury is ionized by an electric arc, producing ultraviolet energy which, in turn, causes a phosphor coating inside the lamp to fluoresce.

Footcandle (fc): unit of illuminance, equal to one lumen per square foot. One footcandle equals 10.76 lux (lx).

Galvanizing: a process by which zinc is deposited on the surface of another metal to improve resistance to corrosion. Steel poles for outdoor lighting are often galvanized for use in corrosive atmospheres.

Glare: excessive brightness.

Globe: a spherical transparent or diffusing enclosure intended to protect a lamp or to diffuse or change the color of its light.

Halogen infrared PAR lamp: a reflector lamp using a halogen capsule inside a PAR enclosure. The capsule is coated to redirect radiant infrared energy back to the filament, thereby increasing lamp efficacy.

Halogen lamp: an incandescent lamp that employs a halogen-gas additive to improve lamp life and efficacy.

High intensity discharge lamp (HID): an electric lamp that produces light directly from an arc discharge under high pressure. Metal halide, high pressure sodium, and mercury vapor are types of HID lamps.

High pressure sodium lamp: an HID lamp in which radiation from sodium vapor under high pressure produces visible light, characterized by a golden-yellow color.

High reactance autotransformer (HX) ballast: a ballast used with HID lamps, consisting of a transformer in the form of primary and secondary coils, used in conjunction with a reactor (a coil wound around an iron core). A capacitor is added across the line for power-factor correction.

IESNA: Illuminating Engineering Society of North America. IESNA is a technical society whose membership is interested in the art, science, and practice of illumination.

Illuminance: luminous flux density, measured in lumens per unit area. Two common units used to measure illuminance are footcandles (lumens per square foot) and lux (lumens per square meter). For conversion purposes, 1 footcandle (fc) is equal to 10.76 lux (lx).

Incandescent lamp: a lamp producing visible radiant energy by electrical heating of a filament.

Initial cost: the cost of buying and installing equipment, exclusive of operating costs such as energy, maintenance, and lamp replacement.

Input power: the total power used by a lamp and ballast, if required, measured in watts.

Instant-start circuit: a circuit used in ballasts for fluorescent lamps. High voltage is applied directly across lamp filaments, causing lamps to start instantaneously. Instant-start circuits start well in cold weather, require low input power, and ignite without lamp flicker.

Intensity: see luminous intensity.

Interval timer: a lighting control that automatically switches a luminaire off after a selected time interval.

Kelvin (K): the standard unit of temperature used in the Systeme Internationale d'Unite (SI) system of measurements. The kelvin scale is used to describe the correlated color temperature of a light source.

Kilowatt-hour (kWh): measure of electrical energy use; the product of power, as measured in kilowatts, and time, as measured in hours. For example, one kilowatt used for one hour equals one kilowatt-hour (kWh).

Lamp: a manufactured light source. For electric lamps, it includes the bulb, the base, and the internal structure that produces light, either a filament or an arc tube. Lamps are often referred to as light bulbs.

Lamp life: see average rated lamp life.

Lens: a glass or plastic element of a luminaire that redirects and controls the distribution of light by refraction.

Light: radiant energy that is capable of producing a visual sensation. The visible portion of the electromagnetic spectrum extends from about 380 to 770 nanometers. See also wavelength.

Light distribution: the spread of light that is produced by a lamp or a luminaire; also the overall pattern of light on a surface.

Light output: luminous flux, measured in lumens. The lumen rating of a lamp is a measure of its total overall light output. See also lumen.

Light pollution: adverse effects, including glare, light tresspass, and sky glow, of unwanted light in the atmosphere, typically produced by the upward components of outdoor lighting systems at night.

Light trespass: extraneous light on adjacent property, typically produced by stray light from outdoor lighting systems. Light trespass includes glare from direct viewing, as well as unwanted "spill light."

Lighting design: the planned application of a lighting system to a space.

Lighting patterns: lighting plans applicable to common spaces and building types.

Lighting system: the equipment used to produce and distribute light, including a luminaire and control system.

Low pressure sodium: a discharge lamp that produces light using a sodium arc in a low pressure atmosphere, characterized by a deep yellow color.

LRC: Lighting Research Center, a multidisciplinary facility for research and education in lighting at Rensselaer Polytechnic Institute.

Lumen: the unit of luminous flux. The lumen is the rate of flow of light, and is used to express the overall light ouput of a lamp.

Lumens per watt (LPW): see efficacy.

Luminaire: a complete lighting unit consisting of a lamp or lamps, together with the parts designed to distribute the light, to position and protect the lamps, and to connect the lamps to a power supply.

Luminance: the photometric quantity most closely associated with the perception of brightness. It is the luminous intensity emitted or reflected in a particular direction per unit area of reflective surface, measured in candelas per square feet or square meters.

Luminance contrast: a measure of the difference in luminance of an object and its background.

Luminous flux: the rate of the flow of light, measured in lumens. The overall light output of a lamp.

Luminous intensity: total luminous flux within a unit solid angle, in units of candelas.

Lux: the Systeme Internationale d'Unite (SI) unit of illuminance equal to 1 lumen per square meter. One lux equals 0.0929 footcandles.

Magnetic ballast: a ballast that uses a magnetic core and coil to provide the voltage, current, and wave form to start the lamp(s) and to maintain operation. See also ballast.

Matte surface: any surface which has a primarily diffuse reflectance.

Maximum to minimum (max:min): the ratio of the maximum illuminance or luminance to the minimum illuminance or luminance found within a lighted area. It is a measures used to indicate lighting uniformity.

Mercury vapor lamp: an HID light source in which radiation from mercury vapor produces visible light, which is characterized by a bluish-white color.

Metal halide lamp: an HID light source in which radiation from a mixture of metallic vapors produces visible light, characterized by a white color.

Motion detector: also called an occupancy sensor, a device that senses the movement of people, animals, and objects using a passive infrared and/or ultrasonic sensor. Motion detectors control other devices, such as luminaires and alarm systems that activate when motion is detected. See also passive infrared and ultrasonic.

Mounting height: the distance from the lamp center within the luminaire to the ground.

NEMA: National Electrical Manufacturers Association. NEMA comprises companies that manufacture electrical equipment, including lighting.

NLPIP: National Lighting Product Information Program. NLPIP is a program of the Lighting Research Center (LRC) at Rensselaer Polytechnic Institute that tests the energy efficiency of lighting technologies and products and produces publications that describe the manufacturer-specific performance characteristics of these technologies.

Occupancy sensor: see motion detector.

Operating cost: see annual operating cost.

Parabolic aluminized reflector lamp (PAR lamp): an incandescent, halogen, or HID lamp with a hard glass bulb, an interior reflecting surface, and a lens to control beam spread.

Passive infrared (motion detector): a technology used in motion detectors to sense a change in the distribution of infrared energy (heat). When a passive infrared sensor detects motion across zones, it activates the device being controlled, such as a luminaire or an alarm. See also motion detector.

Phosphors: chemical compounds that coat the inside of fluorescent and some HID lamps. See also fluorescence.

Photosensor: a device that converts light to electrical current. Photosensors switch lights on or off, based on the amount of incident light.

Polycarbonate: a strong, high-impact plastic material used in luminaires to shield the lamps or to distribute luminous intensity, or both. Polycarbonate shields or refractors are often used to improve the vandal resistance of luminaires. The material will yellow and lose strength when exposed to ultraviolet radiation (UV) for prolonged periods, less so when it has been UV-stabilized.

Power density: a measure of electrical power per unit area, measured in watts per square foot or square meter. Many building codes prescribe maximum power density values for various areas of use in an effort to promote the use of energy-efficient products.

Preheat circuit: a simple electrical circuit used in ballasts for many compact and short linear fluorescent lamps. Preheat circuits are inexpensive and provide a reliable start in cold weather; however, they have low power factors, cannot be dimmed, and produce flashing during lamp ignition.

Quartz halogen lamp: see halogen lamp.

Rated power: the nominal lamp wattage.

Rapid-start circuit: a circuit used in ballasts that preheats the electrodes of fluorescent lamps and then provides for their continuous heating. Advantages over preheat and instant-start circuits include longer lamp life and dimmability. Disadvantages include increased input power, more fragile electrodes, and unreliable starting below 50°F except with low-temperature versions.

Reactor ballast: a ballast for HID lamp operation, consisting of a single coil wound on an iron core, wired in series with the lamp, and a capacitor to increase power factor. Reactor ballasts are typically used for mercury vapor lamps, and when line voltage does not vary more than ± 5 percent.

Rare-earth phosphors: phosphors containing rare-earth elements, which are used in fluorescent lamps to achieve higher efficacy and better color rendering than can be achieved with standard phosphors.

Rated life: see average rated life.

Reflectance: a measure of how effectively a surface diffusely reflects light. Reflectance is the ratio of lumens reflected from a surface to lumens incident upon it.

Reflected glare: excessive brightness from reflections in polished or glossy surfaces in the line of sight.

Reflector: a surface of polished or painted metal, mirrored glass, or metalized plastic shaped to direct light.

Reflector lamps: a class of lamps that have reflecting material integrated into the lamp. Types include common reflector (R), parabolic aluminized reflector (PAR), and multi-faceted reflector (MR) lamps.

Refractor: a device that transmits and redirects the luminous flux from a source. Refractors for outdoor luminaires are typically made from acrylic, polycarbonate, or glass, and when well-designed, help control direct glare.

Restrike time: usually applied to HID light sources, the interval between the extinguishing of an arc and the time it can be reignited.

Screwbase compact fluorescent lamp: a compact fluorescent lamp that has a ballast and a medium screwbase that fits into a standard incandescent lamp socket. A screwbase compact fluorescent lamp may be modular (lamp and ballast are separate pieces) or self-ballasted (lamp and ballast are integrated). Both types are designed to directly replace incandescent lamps.

Sky glow: a result of scattered light in the atmosphere above urban areas.

Slimline lamps: the name for a family of T12 fluorescent lamps operating at 425 milliamperes (mA). These two-pin lamps are designed to operate on instant start circuits, and are most commonly available in 4 and 8-foot lengths. See also instant-start circuit.

Spectra: wavelengths of electromagnetic radiation.

Specular surface: a shiny, mirror-like surface that produces a predominantly directional reflection.

Spot lamp: a lamp that provides a relatively narrow beam of light.

Time clock: a switch designed to automatically turn lights on and off over a daily, weekly, or yearly schedule predetermined by the user.

Timer: see interval timer.

Tungsten halogen lamp: see halogen lamp.

UL: Underwriters Laboratories. An organization that tests electrical components and appliances and lists products that pass safety standards.

Ultrasonic (motion detector): a device that transmits high-frequency vibrations, which are similar to sound waves but above the range of human hearing. These are reflected by objects back to a receiver. Movement produces changes in frequency that are detected and activate a luminaire or alarm.

Ultraviolet (UV) radiation: any radiant energy within the wavelength range of 100 to 400 nanometers (1 nanometer = 1 billionth of a meter, or 1×10^{-9} meters).

Uniformity: in outdoor lighting, a measure indicating how evenly light is distributed across a surface. Typically the measure is expressed as a ratio of one value to another, such as average to minimum, or maximum to minimum. Using ratios, perfect uniformity would be 1:1.

Voltage: the difference in electrical potential that causes current flow in a circuit.

Warm-up time: the time for a light source to reach full light output, often defined by manufacturers as 80 or 90 percent of full light output, after it has been energized.

Watt: unit of real electric power; the rate at which electric energy is used.

Watt-hour: unit of electric energy. One watt-hour is the amount of energy consumed at the rate of 1 watt during a 1-hour period. See also kilowatt-hour.

Wavelength: the distance between two corresponding points of a given wave. Wavelengths of light are measured in nanometers (1 nanometer = 1 billionth of a meter, or 1×10^{-9} meters).

Wind Loading: a rating of the ability of a luminaire and pole to withstand wind. Factors considered include pole height, material, and thickness as well as luminaire size and shape.

Further Reading

Boyce, Peter R. 1991. Security lighting: What we know and what we don't. *Lighting Magazine* 5(6):12-18.

Boyce, P.R., and J.M. Gutkowski. 1995, The if, why and what of street lighting and street crime: a review. *Lighting Research & Technology* 27(2):103-112.

Boyce, P.R., and M.S. Rea. 1990. Security lighting: Effects of illuminance and light source on the capabilities of guards and intruders. *Lighting Research & Technology* 22(2):57-79.

The Electrification Council. Street and Area Lighting Partnership. 1994. *Street and area lighting survey 1994, TEC 888.* [Washington, D.C.]: The Electrification Council.

Ji, Y., and R. Wolsey. 1994. *Lighting answers: Dimming systems for high-intensity discharge lamps.* Troy, NY: Rensselaer Polytechnic Institute.

Leslie, R. P., and K. M. Conway. 1996. *The lighting pattern book for homes.* Troy, NY: Rensselaer Polytechnic Institute.

Maniccia, D., and R. Wolsey. 1994. *Specifier reports: Reflector lamps.* Troy, NY: Rensselaer Polytechnic Institute.

Moyer, J. L. 1992. *The landscape lighting book.* New York: Wiley.

National Lighting Bureau. [1990]. *Lighting and security.* Washington, D.C.: National Lighting Bureau.

National Lighting Product Information Program. 1993. *Specifier reports: Parking lot luminaires.* Troy, NY: Rensselaer Polytechnic Institute.

New England Light Pollution Advisory Group and International Dark-Sky Association. 1995. *Good neighbor outdoor lighting.* Seventh Draft. [s.l.]: New England Light Pollution Advisory Group

Painter, Kate. 1994. The impact of street lighting on crime, fear, and pedestrian street use. *Security Journal.* 5(3):116-124.

Rea, M.S., ed. 1993. *Lighting handbook: Reference & application.* 8th ed. New York, NY: Illuminating Engineering Society of North America.

Index

This book is set in
Goudy Old Style, Bold and Italic
with Helvetica Black and Black Condensed
Book design and production by
Demetrios E. Tonias, P.E.
HMC Group Ltd., Saratoga Springs, NY

Cover art and illustrations of lighting designs by
Mark Patrizio, Waterford, NY
Technology illustrations by
Kaiser Illustrations, Watervliet, NY

Cover design by
Nager Reynolds Design, Westport, Ct

Printed and bound by
Kingsport Press

For a Lighting Research Center catalog, contact:
The Lighting Research Center
Rensselaer Polytechnic Institute
Troy, NY 12180-3590
Facsimile (518) 276-2999, e-mail: lrc@rpi.edu
http://www.lrc.rpi.edu